# Football, Autism & Me

## JOHN O'KANE

EMPIRE
PUBLICATIONS

First published in 2021

EMPIRE PUBLICATIONS
1 Newton Street, Manchester M1 1HW
© John O'Kane 2021

ISBN: 978-1-909360-86-0

# CONTENTS

# ACKNOWLEDGEMENTS

Thank you to everyone who has given their time and effort in the production of this book. This includes friends, former team-mates, managers and colleagues: Eli and Barbara Robinson, Steve Robinson, Paul Gough, Ben Thornley, Lenny Taylor, Pat McGibbon, Stan Ternent, Alan Myers, Andy Bower, Dean Holdsworth, Richie Wellens, Jamie Farrell and Daniel Waterhouse who have all contributed their time, pictures and memories to help tell the story, not to mention playing massive parts in my life in their own ways.

Thank you to my pal Michael Garvey who wrote this with me and definitely makes me read more intelligently; without him my story would probably remain untold. I have pure respect for his patience and guidance in the hours spent helping me make sense of my rants. Also to Wayne Barton, for his help in getting the idea off the ground.

Thank you to Ashley Shaw and all the staff at Empire Publications and to Tony Park and James A. Thomas for their help with stats and pictures.

To my family, for all their help and support over the years. Particularly my mum, who's sadly no longer with us, for fighting so hard to bring me up on her own.

I'd like to dedicate this book to her memory and also to my three kids Taelor, Ruby and Vincent who are mine and Simone's greatest achievements. Here's a little story about your dad…

# INTRODUCTION

MY NAME IS JOHN ANDREW O'KANE, I played football for the biggest club in the world but you probably don't remember me.

I was the right-back in the team that won the FA Youth Cup in 1992, I've shared a pitch with legends like Peter Schmeichel, Roy Keane and Eric Cantona. I've received the hair-dryer treatment from Fergie and partied with the likes of Ryan Giggs and Lee Sharpe. I've roomed with David Beckham and knew him inside out. We did everything together. I then watched as he went on to another level entirely when his career took off whilst my own took me in a completely different direction.

I've played for some of the best (and worst) managers in the game in front of huge crowds in some of the most famous stadiums in the land. I've played in teams that have won league titles, cup finals and narrowly avoided relegation on the last day of the season.

I've never been one to follow the crowd or toe the line. I'm my own person, you get what you see and if I think I'm right I'll argue all day and never be quiet. I know for a fact this hindered my career in an industry where speaking up or questioning authority often means you're out of the door before long.

I've been labelled as laid-back to the point of horizontal, carefree and even lazy by people who didn't really understand me. My team-mates used to call me 'The Spaceman' because it always seemed like I was on my own planet. In my own bubble.

Truth is, I was often battling demons in my head before I even made it out onto the pitch. I was like a swan; calm on the surface but underneath I was flapping like mad trying to suppress stuff that was going on in my head while trying to play football at the same time.

I'm on the autistic spectrum and I suffered from tics and twitches that would get worse in the run up to kick-off as my nerves grew. Managers and team-mates always knew I was a bit twitchy and that there was something different about me, I just tried to get on with it but the stress affected me personally and impacted my football career. It's not an excuse but it didn't help.

Mentally it took a toll on me, I suppressed a lot and it damaged me in the long run. As did battling the feeling that I just didn't belong.

For well over a decade I lived in a superficial bubble known as professional football. It gave me money, fast cars, girls and God knows what else. I've visited different countries flying first-class, met Nelson Mandela and I'm probably one of the least famous people to have switched on Blackpool Illuminations but it just wasn't me and it didn't make me happy. I always felt that I was different and I was always fighting it. I was battling this feeling in my head that I didn't belong there and that I was destined to do something else. In the end it got too much and I had to get out.

It wasn't an injury, age or a managerial decision that ended my football career - I did. Most players are at their peak in their late twenties but for me it was just a job and I needed a career change. I burst the bubble and walked away.

I took a step out into the real world, I worked in

an office, on building sites, in care homes and schools. I worked 18-hour shifts wiping backsides and gained more self-worth and respect from my family than I ever got from football, whilst rediscovering my love of the game playing non-league, a world away from the bright lights of Old Trafford. I became a dad to three great kids. The greatest job of them all.

Sorry to disappoint but this isn't another book about some guy who didn't make it at Manchester United nor does it pay homage to the 'Class of 92'. People have different paths in life and I've found mine.

This is my story.

# THE ACCIDENTAL FOOTBALLER

I NEVER REALLY HAD AN AVID INTEREST in football growing up nor did I watch professional games as a kid. That may sound strange considering what I ended up doing as a career. My local club, Nottingham Forest, were one of the biggest clubs in the country at the time but I was far too busy playing out with my mates to follow a team or watch a game on TV.

We played football in the street like most kids did but other activities like knock-a-door-run, hedge hopping or chasing girls were just as, if not more, important.

I grew up in a council house in the Bilborough area of Nottingham with my mum, nana and Grandad 'Poppa'. Our house was very small but the estate we lived on was great. The image of a council estate today probably makes people think of poverty but back then it was the norm as not a lot of people could afford to buy their own homes. I've been back since and the area has become run-down over time, like a lot of them have, but growing up there it felt like paradise.

I had a happy childhood with some great memories. I didn't have a father figure, just my Uncle Jim who was the only real consistent male presence around. He was a decent guy who was always there for us and I was quite close to his daughter, my cousin Vanessa, growing up.

My grandad worked down the pit and then would be in the pub after he clocked off. He was everything to me, the bee's knees, and my earliest memory is being sat on his knee watching Muhammad Ali fight on the TV because he loved boxing. I always remember the smell of alcohol on him when he got home and if I try hard enough, I can still smell it now. It was only later in life that I realised that he was an alcoholic.

In my eyes he was perfect but then years later I found out that wasn't the case from my mum and Uncle Jim. They had no money growing up and he used to spend all of it in the pub meaning they had to go without and the family was very poor. My mum also has two sisters, Margaret who lives in Australia and Maureen in Bournemouth, they all say that they had a tough upbringing but I was sheltered from it.

My mum lived and breathed for me, she had at least four jobs and worked her backside off just to give me as much as she could. She always used to bring something home for me, even if it was just a little bag of Lego. She was a machinist for a while, then a cleaner, all were low-paid jobs with no security.

She had no education and left school at 12 or 13, she was a redhead and you didn't mess with her because she was an absolute one-off. I have inherited her sense of right and wrong in that I'm quite black and white with no grey areas, I think it's a good trait to have. I can be diplomatic but if I think I'm right I will fight for it and I don't care who you are; Fergie or anybody. She was also a very good natural athlete which is where I get my sporting ability.

We're also both hot-headed, if I feel like I've been wronged I'm like a bull in a china shop. It takes a lot to get into my circle and if you hurt someone within it, you're getting blasted and she was exactly the same. I always tell my kids that if you think you're right then never be quiet, don't be a sheep and anyone who knows me in football will tell you that I've never followed the crowd.

I was a happy-go-lucky lad who could do no wrong in her eyes and she would have killed for me. One incident which springs to mind is when we were playing knock-a-door run on the estate. I knocked on someone's door, knowing that it would aggravate them and smashed a pane in the window when I threw a stone. They chased me with a plank of wood and smacked me over the head with it. I went crying to my mum, I'd have been about seven or eight at the time and swore blind I'd not done anything. She went round there and smashed all their windows. I never admitted to her that I did do it or she would have killed me.

Another time she'd gone to bingo with my nana and left me with the next-door neighbours. I was messing about while they were cutting their hedge with the old school trimmers which were razor-sharp and I kept putting my fingers in the hedge as their daughter was doing it. Next thing I just remember screaming and my uncle was taking me to hospital with my hand in a bag. The top ends of my fingers were literally hanging by a thread and had to be sewn back on. I remember having four needles in between my fingers and thinking I was going to die, it was a pretty traumatic experience to be fair. I thought my mum was going to kill our neighbours but this time, given the circumstances, I told her the truth that it was my fault.

Another time I fell into a full row of nettles with stings covering my whole body. I remember having vinegar poured all over me and being given the standard bottle of Lucozade for recovery so I had my fair share of accidents growing up. My mum was always there for me though, no matter how much trouble I'd got myself into, she always wanted me to be happy and I had a good upbringing.

As for my dad, I didn't meet him until I was about 20 when I was just starting to get into the United first team, his name is Hugo Lyn but growing up there wasn't any mention of him. He and my mum were never together as far as I know and it may have just been a one-night stand or a fling. I never spoke to her about it until I met him but when we did I had no feelings for him whatsoever because I'd not missed anything.

I met him at a reserve game away at Nottingham Forest, it was all pre-arranged and when I got off the coach we shook hands. They watched the game and we went to a pub afterwards where we played pool and I met his partner and my half-sister. I took my ex-girlfriend and a mate there, not wanting to go on my own because it was awkward.

I always wonder why he chose to get in touch then when I was playing for United. That may be cynical and it could well have been organised by my mum who may have thought that it was time that I met him. He's Jamaican-Chinese so I'm mixed-race and I've been told that my nana and poppa wouldn't allow him to see me, he kept saying that it wasn't his fault. He didn't fight for me though, he gave up and took the easy option.

I've met him a few times and he seems like a lovely guy, very laid-back with an afro and he still lives in Nottingham as far as I know. I've never delved into my roots or ever wanted to but I probably have a large Jamaican or Chinese family somewhere which I've missed out on because he didn't want to fight for me - I've never forgiven him for that.

I was always craving that traditional family set-up when I was a kid. My mate Robbo, Steve Robinson, who I played with for Pheasant Colts and who went on to play for a few clubs in the Football League including Birmingham City, had the perfect family in my eyes. He had another sibling and his parents were the coaches of our team.

I had another best mate called Lenny Sharpe who lived across the road from me on the estate and we were like brothers because for at least ten years we did everything together. We were a pair of rascals who would terrorise the estate from eight in the morning until it was time for us to go in at night which was usually when the street lights came on. He was a great lad, there's too many memories to mention but he says he remembers stuff like me dropping the cheese and onion soup that his dad had made me and my mum catching him singing 'Oh Vienna' at the top of his voice at one of my birthday parties. Great times.

I lost touch with him eventually when I moved away and he's tried a few times to organise a meet up but it gets more difficult as you get older with having kids and everything else. In a way, I'd just like to remember him as he was because we made some great memories together growing up and it would be great to go back to those times just for a day.

He had a brother and a couple of sisters and I was jealous as hell of them having that family unit. They would always go to the pub and I would go with them. I always wanted to be at someone else's house and be part of that environment, the security of having a dad there. I didn't have that, when my mum went to work I had no siblings to mess around with. As an only child I was quite lonely, wishing I had a brother or sister.

I played out with my mates all the time but when I went in at the end of the day I was bored. There was nothing to do apart from watch TV, which I'm still addicted to now as that's what I was brought up on, similar to the way that kids have iPads now. I just played out then watched TV.

Holidays would be in Skegness, we never went abroad because we couldn't afford to. I always remember a bus would turn up at the end of the road and the whole street would get on it. It was quality and to me it was just like going abroad, everybody went there. I also used to spend a week in Blackpool every summer because my Auntie Maureen and Uncle John lived there. I was quite close to my cousins Lisa and Paul, who was a little bit older than me and a good kid, we all had some good times together.

Sadly, tragedy struck when I was about ten and Paul was killed in a house fire. He managed to save the rest of the family but died in the process, I was only young but it was a very sad time in the family and I'm not sure my auntie and uncle have ever really got over it.

At school I was mischievous. I was very bright and always wanted to do my work on time; I'd rush it, always wanting to be first. Me and a girl called Alison Bellshaw were the stars of our year. We were both sporty and fancied each other as well, always competing against each other to see who could get work done first.

My teacher would say I was always the first one to disrupt the class, it may have been a tic or an anxiety thing and I can't remember why I wanted to talk so much but I would get my work done and then disrupt everyone else. A bit like my eldest lad now. I wouldn't say that I was academic but I probably should have done more than I did.

My tics first started when I was about six because I used to blink almost constantly and my mum used to tell me off for it. She got me a pair of glasses but that didn't work and it was never really picked up on at school or in football later on. People just knew that I was a bit twitchy and in my head I always knew I was wired up a little bit differently to everyone else.

It can take various forms and a lot of people are on the spectrum. People with similar conditions will understand exactly what I mean when I say it's caused by a chemical imbalance in your head, that feeling that you need to do a twitch or a certain movement and you won't be satisfied until you've done it. It could have been triggered by an early trauma or it could be hereditary, I've no idea.

Kids can be cruel but I largely got away with it in terms of bullying, even with the twitches. I was popular, good at sport and if someone had a go I would laugh it off or tear them to bits. It was a similar story where racism was concerned because I was a mixed-race kid in a predominantly white area, although I did experience it to a degree.

I got called 'Paki' quite a bit which was the insult of choice in those days. Kids wouldn't bat an eyelid about using the word 'nigger' but I classed myself as white because I'd been brought up in a white household. People saw me as being white as well because of the mates I hung around with and I didn't speak with an accent. I was just 'John' to a lot of the people who knew me and I was a strong character.

I was brainwashed in a way, not knowing who I was or where I came from. I'm aware of what black people have had to go through in the past and the issue of racism in today's society. I never really experienced racism whilst playing football but I have massive respect for the likes of Viv Anderson and John Barnes; what they went through laid the foundations for the players of my generation and today, although recent events have shown that there's still work to do.

Eventually we moved out of my grandparents as my

mum and nana used to clash a lot and I remember them having a massive argument and us leaving with bags in our hands. After that we lived in bedsits and at one point lived above a hotel in Sherwood. We were proud people and hid it well but during that time we probably lived in about a dozen different places. I felt like a gypsy, we lived on a caravan park at one stage which had its own water park. We were flat broke, just wheeling and dealing to get by which was never boring but it wasn't long until we were on the move again and I must have had about four or five different schools. We moved everywhere.

I resented my mum for not having a settled job like my mates' parents had, we were always on the move and I hated the lifestyle. I was moving schools and having to make new friends all the time, I was protected from it to an extent but it was draining. I never complained to her face though, I just had to get on with it.

She got married when I was about eleven to my step-dad Pete Barratt who's a good guy. He did everything for me, taking me all over the country for football and working his backside off. We didn't have much money and I always remember one time when we were going on tour with Pheasant Colts I had no football kit. He worked the whole night to pay for it and get it for the next morning, it was an England kit and it was quality.

I always respected him but made his life hell, as most stepsons do in that situation. My mum would always take my side and I remember they used to argue a lot over me because I would mess around and knew I could get away with it. I appreciated him though and he was like the rock that I'd been missing, I told him that later in life.

I never had the football vibe growing up. I started playing on the street, played for a few local teams and then ended up at Manchester United, it's mad really when you think about it. I didn't have a dad to take me to watch Forest or County. I just played the game and didn't realise that there were leagues or anything organised. Nottingham Forest won two European Cups under Brian Clough when I was growing up but I never went to see them once, we just weren't a football family.

I never watched it on TV and didn't go to an actual game until I was about 14 when I went to see Forest play Liverpool at the City Ground. I remember watching Liverpool who had John Barnes, Ray Houghton and Ronnie Whelan playing for them at the time and thinking, "Fuck me they're good." I'd seen nothing like it. It was unbelievable.

I was a street footballer – you don't see many players like that anymore but that was how I learnt the game. There were no academies in those days, I just played out on the street and that's what gave me my identity as a player. There were no referees, if I got whacked I had to get up and get on with it because I knew that if I went in my mum would probably keep me there.

I loved it but it's not the same nowadays with more cars on the road and dodgy people knocking around. You can't let your own kids play out freely like we used to. We used to play against two double gates that were opposite each other and would be out all day. It was a tiny space but to us it was like Wembley.

I played in my school team and my mate Mark Lees got me involved with playing for the Boy Scouts where a coach from a local club called Rise Park Jets came and asked if I wanted to play for them. I think I'd played for the Scouts against them and absolutely blitzed them, I stayed with them for a year before moving on to Rise Park

9

Rockets and then Pheasant Colts where I began to realise that I was half-decent.

My Uncle Jim was a qualified referee and did some of our games at Pheasant, we were a good side and we won almost every game we played and began to attract a few scouts. There were a few lads there who made it professionally such as Matt Carbon, Paul McGregor (who played for Forest), Michael Galloway, Lee Marshall and my mate Steve Robinson. We were very successful and I would play all over the pitch depending on where I was deemed to be most effective. If the opposition had a star player I would often play directly against them because the coaches knew I could handle it.

## Eli and Barbara Robinson - Pheasant Colts

*John joined Pheasant Colts junior football team at the age of 10, he quickly made friends with our son Steven and they are still close friends to this day. The team's successes and the football produced by them was a joy to behold, in the Barcelona style of 'Tippy Tappy' football, gradually changing as the game became more physical. The inevitable happened when six of the lads, including John, went on to be professional footballers.*

*John was always calm, mature in his play and very skilled. He was quiet verbally but he led the defence brilliantly and his talent meant he could play in any position asked of him. When he was 14 I remember him getting sent off for swearing at the referee, however the ref had got it wrong because it was aimed at our son Steven!*

*John moved around quite a bit so our telephone number for him was constantly updating but thankfully we never lost him. He used to moan every time we had to walk anywhere, he hated it unless there was a ball at his feet.*

*It's a pleasure to know him and to have followed his football career along with all the other professionals that came from our junior side. A top talent and genuine person.*

## Steve Robinson – Former Pheasant Colts, Birmingham City and Swindon Town

*I've known John for 34 years. It's a long time, a bit too long really.*

*He was playing for a Rise Park team and we went to play them and some of their lads ended up coming to us. From then we were always pretty close, a bit like brothers really. We could fall out pretty easily but we'd soon make up. We had that kind of relationship and I think he knew he could rely on me.*

*We had a great side and six of us from that team went on to play professional football which for a little kid's team in Nottingham is quite unbelievable really. We won everything up until the age of about 15. We'd pass it and knock it around and it was a special team to be a part of.*

*You know when one of those lads shoots up as a teenager and is taller than everybody else? Well that was John. He became a very good central defender and was like a Rolls-Royce, cruising and taking his time at the back. It was pretty obvious that he was class and football came very easily to him.*

*When John moved to Manchester at 15 to do his last year at school there he'd still come back for the odd game which says a lot about him. I think he enjoyed Pheasant Colts as much as he enjoyed anything he did in his career.*

I got spotted by both Forest and County playing for Nottingham Boys and flitted between the two. At County Jimmy Sirrel ran the training on a Thursday night, he'd managed the club and was probably in his seventies by then. That was my introduction to a proper coaching set-up. We'd be put through drills, how to move, awareness and how to turn. I was a street player but the rawness and determination were there. County illicitly made me sign something which turned out to be a year's contract and my mum went barmy. I was told later that she went down there and ripped it up, she left the final decision on where to go up to me and didn't push me in any particular direction.

I remember being in Brian Clough's office at Forest with him telling me he wanted me to sign but I was very laid-back about it, I just wanted to play football. Arsenal were also interested but I didn't fancy London. By that point I was playing Sunday League for a team called Oadby Town juniors when Nobby Stiles came to watch me. I think I played up-front and scored a hat-trick that day. I had absolutely no idea who he was or that he'd won the World Cup. I just remember my mum saying that he wanted to speak to me.

He was a little old man with a bald head wearing a United coat and he asked if I wanted to go for a trial at the Cliff playing against England under-18s. It was around the time when Fergie had sent his scouts to find the best kid in every area of the country and I was probably the best in Nottingham within my age group at the time.

I went up and played centre-half in the game, which I usually hated because I felt that it restricted me, but I could play anywhere and it suited me to have the game in front of me so I could read it. I remember Giggsy played and Steve Robinson was there as well but only got on for a few minutes so wasn't really given a fair crack of the whip.

I had a brilliant game and read everything, apart from one moment when the ball was kicked from their keeper, it bounced in front of me and went over my head. I was devastated, the one mistake I'd made and I was convinced they wouldn't sign me after that.

Luckily it didn't put them off and Fergie took me

to his house to get me to sign and we played snooker. I remember him saying to me, "If you sign for us, we'll look after you and make you a player."

I didn't know a lot about the history of the club, my earliest memories of United are of failure, that team with Strachan, Robson and Remi Moses. An attacking side that was decent but always fell short. The day after the trial they took us to the game at Old Trafford where the first team were playing Arsenal. Michael Knighton was in talks to buy the club and famously ran on the pitch bouncing the ball on his head. Neil Webb had just signed and we won 4-1.

The place blew me away, climbing those steps and seeing the pitch beneath me. That feeling. It was the old Stretford End then, all standing and not like it is now but it took your breath away. Then there was the noise and the sheer number of people. I realised then the size of the club and that it was on a different level to anything I'd experienced before.

It was overwhelming and I was always going to sign from that moment. I fell in love with Manchester United then and I'm still a fan to this day.

## PIZ BUIN

I SPENT MY FIRST YEAR AS A UNITED PLAYER travelling between Nottingham and Manchester in school holidays before moving up in the summer of 1990 and finishing my education at Cheadle Hulme High School. My schoolwork suffered after signing for United, I didn't study for my exams, sat them and got nothing.

I moved into digs on Bury New Road with Paul Gough, Sean McAuley, Raphael Burke, Lenny Taylor and we were soon joined by a lad called David Beckham. I was there for about two years before me and Becks moved down the road to a lady called Eva Cody.

A few of the other lads were homesick to begin with but it never really affected me. It was cliquey among all the apprentices and young players though, the Manchester lads stuck together, as did the lads from Scotland or Ireland so me and Becks ended up becoming close, maybe because we were a bit more 'southern' than the rest with him having come up from London.

We were best mates who lived in each other's pockets and did everything together. We had the same tastes in clothes and fashion. We'd meet girls together and even shared them, although at the time we were two teenagers who were both a bit wet behind the ears so it stayed fairly innocent for those wondering.

When you live with someone for an extended period of time and sleep in the same room together you get to know them as a person and I knew Becks inside out. We'd often lie on our beds, talking about what our futures would be like when we made it at United and I still say that he owes me a million pounds... I can still see it now, he had a big mirror at the bottom of his bed and I can remember being sat in front of it on a Sunday afternoon rocking on a chair and saying to him, "Where do you reckon we're going to be in five years' time?"

"I'm going to be playing for Man United," came the reply. He was so sure that was what he was going to be doing. We agreed then that if only one of us made it we'd give the other a million pounds and we shook on it so Becks, on the off chance that you're reading this, I'll send you my bank details!

David Beckham was made for United and I've never seen a footballer so driven. I think he is underrated and I loved watching him play because he could play Hollywood passes and was an excellent crosser of the ball. He was a perfectionist and a bit of a flash cockney who loved his clothes, hair gels and always had the latest boots but he turned into a Manc. People like Nicky Butt didn't like him because he was everything Butty wasn't, he did everything as well as Beckham but didn't have that Hollywood pass. Becks was flash and people like Butty and Karl Brown, who were from tough areas of Manchester, couldn't relate to that and saw through it.

Now he can hold a room because of who he is but back in the day Becks couldn't hold a conversation like Robbie Savage could for example. We got each other though and bounced off one another. We were pushed together because of the digs and we both used to take the piss out of Gary Neville. Becks loved a challenge and always wanted to test himself, which is why he didn't stay at United and went on to play all over the world. He's been very clever in the way he branded himself and he homed in on that image.

The rest, as they say, is history. We drifted apart in the end after he became established in the first team and he gravitated towards Neville who was best man at his wedding. People have different paths and he just went on to another level, although I have often wondered if he was told to keep away from me because I was seen as trouble or a bad influence.

If I met him tomorrow, we'd talk and laugh about old times. I did see him at the reunion for the Class of 92 film and got a nice picture with him and my lad but I've not been in contact with him since I left the club. It's a shame we never kept in touch but you move on with your life and that's what he did.

The life of an apprentice at the biggest club in the world was quite repetitive and it was a tough environment in which to learn. We wouldn't just train and play football, we were given various jobs to do around the Cliff to help with the upkeep of the place. This would include cleaning boots or helping with the laundry. I used to clean the gym and that was the worst one to do; all the dust, sweat, the floor and the mirrors. It would take ages and if it wasn't perfect when Eric Harrison inspected he'd keep us there even longer, it was like being in the Army.

We'd be there most of the day but if we got off early, we used to play snooker or go shopping but when you're earning about £30 a week you can't really go mad. I was decent at snooker though and none of the other lads could beat me. My mum had worked in a pub when I was younger and I remember playing pool against all the old men so my hand-eye coordination must have stemmed from there. Once I worked out how to play snooker I was lethal and the other lads didn't stand a chance!

You'd go back to the digs and try and fill the rest of the day, Goughy would be on his guitar, Becks would be folding his clothes or doing his hair and Raph would be in his pit. We'd then go down for tea - that's if we ate it. Sometimes we used to pick it up with toilet paper and flush it away because it was horrible. I remember refusing to eat stuff on a few occasions which never went down well with the landlady. Sometimes in the evening you went out for a bit then came back, went to bed and it would all start again.

On a Sunday morning we'd all sit round the kitchen table whilst the landlady cooked us a fry-up. She'd be stroking the Alsatian dog she had and then peel the bacon out of the packet to put under the grill. We'd be crying inside because you could see the dog hair that had come off her hands whilst it was cooking and we used to howl with laughter when we saw who had got it in their breakfast!

## Paul Gough – Manchester United Youth Player 1988-1992

*Me and John became good friends as we were both placed in the same digs on Bury New Road and today I count him as one of my best mates. At that time, there were about three houses that were all walking distance to the Cliff providing digs for the boys who weren't from Greater Manchester. The club paid the landlady £60 per week and in return there was an adult looking in on the house and we got breakfast and an evening meal with lunch at the training ground. I got the impression that the landladies were doing it on the cheap so they could make more on the £60 per player they were looking after.*

*The food started off like a hotel, at first there was everything for breakfast but as time went on it was a few cereals and toast.*

*Evening meals got worse too, if you didn't eat it you had two options – toast for supper or go to the garage for sweets. Nothing like what young players have access to today with the army of support staff covering sports science, diet, etc.*

*Fergie would call in every now and then for 5 minutes after he finished at the Cliff just to do a check and his presence was enough for everyone to be on their best behaviour.*

*Once we were full-time, after training we did what most young lads did before the PlayStation generation. We'd walk back to digs for tea, banter, TV, banter, then went to bed listening to music. I remember sharing a room with John and Becks when we were 16 listening to Simply Red and Prince albums in the main and taking turns on playing CDs before falling asleep.*

Among the rest of the lads I was a big character and a good player so I was accepted. I was probably a bit arrogant but nothing or nobody scared me. The older lads used to bully us though and a lot of the stories about what went on have been well documented.

Giggsy was the main ringleader but the second-year apprentices or young pros did their fair share. We'd train, have our dinner and then have about an hour or so spare in the early afternoon where it would all start. There would be mock trials if you'd supposedly done something wrong or you'd have to lie on a bench, pinned down, putting your head below it whilst a ball was smashed in your face.

Chatting up and shagging the mop was another, you'd have to show all your moves and if it wasn't good enough you'd be laughed at. Another game involved skateboarding up to one of the other lads to chat them up or tell jokes. I remember having the United kit painted on me in dubbin with a wire brush whilst stood naked in a bath, I slipped and caught my foot under the tap. I was out for several weeks after that and still have the scar to show for it now.

It was cruel and some lads struggled with it, Becks was one who was always on-guard and some of the others used to go and hide in the gym to avoid it. A few of the lads like Nicky Butt or Karl Brown would flat out refuse to be forced into doing anything and no one would mess with either of them because they were hard as nails. Robbie Savage used to love it and would be in his element which I'm sure isn't a surprise to anybody reading this.

It didn't stop at the Cliff either, another one was lads in the digs being lined up to watch a porn film to see if they got a hard on. I remember being stood there and asked:

"How many holes does a girl have?"

"Well there's two isn't there?"

"Nah mate there's three, there's another one just above the fanny, it's called a... Piz Buin!"

I found out later that Piz Buin is actually a brand of sun cream, there must have been a bottle of it in the room at the time, I still use it when I go on holiday now.

I remember me and Becks being forced to fight each other for the entertainment of the other lads. I was a big lad then so just put him in a headlock and took him to the ground. He was quite small before he sprung up to six foot two in the space of a year or so.

It was bullying, no question about it, but it built character and that's why we ended up being so successful. Nowadays they'd call it abuse and some players were tortured but in a way it was endorsed by the coaches. They were fully aware of it and allowed it to happen.

At Christmas they would clear all the chairs and tables in the canteen and the younger players would be forced to act out some sort of play for the first team and coaching staff's entertainment. It could be something like *Snow*

*White and the Seven Dwarves* or maybe the nativity. I starred in it one year but I can't remember what as, it was brutal though and not an enjoyable experience. I remember certain lads would refuse to take part. My acting career was short-lived thankfully but it just goes to show the sort of stuff we were put through and how these humiliating traditions were upheld by the people at the top, all with the justification that it was tradition or good for team spirit.

Our game time would come in the 'A' or 'B' team on a Saturday morning. Nobby Stiles and Jimmy Curran would take the 'B' team while Eric Harrison was in charge of the 'A' team. I liked Nobby and felt that he understood me as a player and where my strengths lay, probably because he'd scouted me in the first place. He knew I would make a good defender because of the way I read the game and made it look easy.

He was an angry man but also very funny. He used to froth at the mouth like a Rottweiler if we weren't up to standard in a game. His eyes used to bulge but he knew who could take it and who couldn't. He was a winner and would say things like, "Get one goal, get another. Don't feel sorry for anybody!"

We used to beat teams like Liverpool 4-0 or 5-0 and still he wouldn't be happy. They were probably still the most successful team at the time and were all about keeping the ball, pass and move. United's philosophy was to express yourself with no fear and attack and that's what's been lost a little bit now.

Nobby wanted us to score ten every game and I suppose that's what made him a World Cup winner who we all respected massively. Losing was unacceptable, he instilled the fear of defeat in us. We were genuinely scared of losing and it was a bullying mentality that was employed by the coaches. You had to play at your best and I felt from the age of 14 to 18 I kind of peaked.

At the time I loved the whole football life, I loved the scene and playing under the pressure. No one ever took the piss out of me for my tics because I was a good player and they respected me. Although the other lads always knew that I was a bit twitchy.

We never really mixed with the first team but Bryan Robson would come and talk to us about the values of the club and the levels you needed to be at. It was drummed into you that you played for the badge and that United were a special club who every team wanted to beat so you had to try that bit harder.

Reminders of the size and history of the club were all around. I remember going to Old Trafford on a Friday afternoon to pick up my wages which would involve walking past Sir Matt Busby's office, the door would always be open and you'd see him in there puffing away on his cigar. He'd wave as we walked past, "Alright boys?"

My knowledge of footballing history still wasn't extensive but over time I learned who he was and what he did for the club. They'd kept him around and you'd see Bobby Charlton pop into the dressing room after the odd youth game. We'd go to Northern Ireland to play in the Milk Cup where we'd stay in Harry Gregg's hotel and sit and listen to him tell us stories about the Busby Babes. He was great with us and showed what it meant to play for Manchester United and what we were representing every time we took to the pitch.

The standard of young players at the club at the time was very high but I always felt that I held my own and was up there with the best. I was a big lad for my age and I regularly played in the 'A' team with the older lads who

I got on well with like Alan Tonge and Pete Smyth, I still speak to both of them now. I got in the squad for the FA Youth Cup a year early in 1990/91 and came on as a sub in the semi-final against Sheffield Wednesday at Hillsborough playing against lads who were at least a year or two older but it didn't faze me.

## Ben Thornley – Manchester United 1988-98

*I've known John since we were 14 and attended a trial for England schoolboys at Trent Polytechnic. I was thinking what a real classy player he was. He had all the attributes to be a top-class centre-half and being from Nottingham people were quick to make comparisons with Des Walker which continued throughout his career. He read the game, he was quick, strong and had two very good feet. I was very surprised when the list of lads was whittled down that he didn't get through to the next phase.*

*After that we sporadically came across each other at United where I was part of the schoolboy set-up and John would come up to train and play in the school holidays. It was the same situation with David Beckham, Keith Gillespie and Robbie Savage who were also from further afield.*

*We both got into the squad for the FA Youth Cup a year early in 1990/91 and got on the pitch in the semi-final against Sheffield Wednesday at Hillsborough. I remember Nobby Stiles and even Alex Ferguson being very complimentary after the game and it goes to show how highly they thought of us at a time when we were both still at school.*

*Where I played for Salford Boys was literally a stone's throw away from the Cliff training ground so you used to get people keeping tabs on us. Scouts from United would amble down to watch us when we were at home whereas I'm not sure John had that exposure where he was from so it was an even bigger achievement for him to be involved at that time.*

★

Ryan Giggs was the star of that youth team and he was the young player supporters were talking about at the time. He was a genius and almost unplayable. I used to have to mark him in training which stood me in good stead and while he never embarrassed me he was jinky and like a gazelle. I always felt he was at his peak in those early years and then he maintained a high level throughout the rest of his career. Ryan was a complete freak of nature.

I remember playing in a youth tournament in France at full-back behind him and I tried to overlap him a couple of times and got absolutely slaughtered for it. Brian Kidd was screaming from the touchline, "Pass him the ball! Leave him, let him do it himself!"

Ryan had girls flocking around him even at that age. I remember watching him on the dancefloor when we used to go out and he had so much confidence, probably because he'd had to grow up quicker than the rest of us due to his involvement with the first team. He was on a different level on and off the pitch. Pound for pound he's probably the best United player of all time in terms of appearances made and the number of trophies won. A legend.

But while Giggsy was destined for greatness there were other lads who at the time were on a similar level but never became established either because of injury or because their face didn't fit. Adrian Doherty played on the opposite side to Ryan and was considered just as good at the time. He didn't look like a footballer though, I remember seeing this kid walk in wearing a pair of ripped grey school trousers, laces undone and a scruffy grey jumper but when he put his kit on he was out of this world.

He was fearless with the pace of Kanchelskis and the

craft of Giggsy. He was small but tough, I used to wince at some of the challenges he would throw himself into. He stood out a mile and has almost legendary status among the players who were at the club at that time.

He lived with a family over in Ancoats and would go out busking on the streets. He was a lovely lad and completely unique. He didn't really buy into the whole football bubble; he turned up, played and went home to do his own thing. Him and Colin McKee were good mates and I remember going out with them a few times, he would sit down with his drink, get his guitar out and start playing, that was his life and everyone loved him.

He got a bad injury before he could play in the first team which stopped him progressing and I just remember him drifting in and out of rooms, like a ghost. It's very sad what happened to him in the end as he died young but I prefer to remember him as he was. I can still see him now, stood on the right wing at Littleton Road ready to receive the ball and take players on. He was awesome and would have had no problems cutting it in the first team.

My housemate Raphael Burke was another pacy right-winger who had played for England schoolboys. He was a hell of a player who was regarded as a future star but often struggled in big games and was given a hard time by the coaches. The old school mentality was that players like him had a chip on their shoulder, he was a bit flash in the way he dressed and was belittled constantly. He had all the makings of a top player but the club didn't look after him and he struggled in that tough environment.

Jules Maiorana was another winger who was a bit older and had already played a few games in the first team. He was capable of producing flashes of brilliance and was very brave. He used to get smashed because he was quite fancy on the ball, but he would ride tackles and would have been some player if he hadn't have got injured. Jules was a great individual player who would get the ball and take three or four players on, like George Best. I remember watching him playing for the reserves and it was ridiculous how strong and powerful he was. He was so fast and quite tall and leggy for a winger.

He was another free spirit who didn't really fit the mould with his dark Italian hair and was similar to me in that he'd been brought up to have his own mind. He had a lot of problems with his knee and then just disappeared, as was the norm with players who fell by the wayside. You train with them every day and then one day they're just gone, it's a brutal business.

Karl Brown was as good as Nicky Butt but a bit smaller, he got a bad injury and wasn't given the opportunity to come back from it. He's now a coach at United, he could tackle and was as tough as Keano. I'm still in contact with him now and he came to my wedding, a good lad.

Paul Gough remains one of my best mates to this day, he played a bit like Ray Wilkins and was two-footed but wasn't enough like a Nicky Butt type of player in Eric Harrison's eyes. He could ping a ball and run for England but wasn't very quick. He had this very up-right running style and was always having problems with his back which finished him in the end and the club paid him off. He was a clever lad and went into Law, doing a degree and now has his own business in Newcastle.

It was Goughy who gave me my nickname as well, 'Scone' (as in gone) - I've no idea where it came from, maybe because I was quite quick. Even now at reunions the likes of Giggsy still greet me with, "Alright Scone?"

Fergie was always a visible presence around the club

and made time for everyone's parents. He knew everything about everybody. I don't know how he did it but I loved the attention to detail. Years later my mum was working at Stockport train station when he just came up to her and said, "Alright Rita, how's John doing?"

I was taken along to Rotterdam in May 1991 for the European Cup Winners' Cup final against Barcelona with the rest of the youth and reserve players. Some of the lads got quite boozy and I remember Ralph Milne having a fight on the bus, he threw a can of beer at someone's head and left the club not long after.

That was the best atmosphere I've witnessed at a game, *Sit Down* by James was a popular song at the time and the whole stadium was singing it. Barcelona were a great side with Ronald Koeman at the back and he scored a great free kick from about 40 yards out. We were the underdogs but Mark Hughes scored twice to win it and cap a memorable night.

The club was turning a corner and joining in with the celebrations that evening I didn't realise that I would play my own part in its future success a lot sooner than expected.

# THE REAL CLASS OF '92

I WAS PART OF ONE OF THE GREATEST YOUTH teams of all time, but in recent years it has been used to create a brand which has almost taken on a life of its own. The 'Class of '92' brand has grown legs since the release of the film and been used to launch a business empire which has included a football club, hotels, property and even a university.

I had a bit-part in the making of the film with the rest of the other lads, but we didn't really get much recognition. At the première in London it was all about the 'big six' and we were just a sideshow. They had their own private booth whilst the rest of us mingled with ordinary folk.

I've seen the film and it's a decent watch but I think they should have called it the 'Class of '99' or something because the title is misleading and plays down the role some of us who didn't go on to become established in the first team played in winning that youth cup.

There's this perception that those six players all came through at the same time and went on to conquer all-comers almost on their own. It's been talked about as if they were the second coming of the Busby Babes, but they were surrounded by great players like Schmeichel, Irwin, Keane and Cantona who helped pull them through or made them look better when they'd not had the best game. Trust me I know, I should have been one of them.

I will never be bitter about what those lads went on to achieve, winning numerous trophies and doing the treble, because they worked hard for it. I supported them like every other United fan but it's often forgotten that most of us in that team played for the first team before carving out decent careers in the game.

Basing it on the 1992 FA Youth Cup winning side alone it's a bit of a myth as well. Of the six players that the film focused on, only Gary Neville, Becks and Butty were regulars in that team. Giggsy was already involved in the first team by that point and only played when he wasn't needed there or in the important games. Phil Neville was a couple of years younger and Scholesy couldn't get in the side at that time because we had such a strong group.

You've got to respect the culture of bringing players through at United because they've been the best in the country at doing it going back to the days of Sir Matt Busby. It benefited us back then playing in the 'A' and 'B' teams on a Saturday morning rather than the current system of under-18's and under-23's because we were playing against men at a young age and some brutal sides such as Tranmere, Carlisle and Marine.

I remember going to play at Marine for the 'A' team, their team was filled with Scousers who would always be up for a fight against the dreaded Mancs. Winning the battle first and not letting them bully us was always key. It changed with the introduction of academies but if you're not in and around the first team by the age of 22 or 23 then you're never going to be, something I was to learn for myself later.

The side for the Youth Cup games was more or less the 'A' team that played together every week but those were the games I wanted to play in. We were led by Eric Harrison who was old school but everything I think that a coach should be, he saw absolutely everything. We used to call him 'Der Führer.' He was a great coach and was there at the right time; he'd brought Mark Hughes and Norman Whiteside through but his methods were nothing like Pep Guardiola, it was basic but that team made it look revolutionary because we were good players driven by the fear of losing which had been instilled in us.

We all had good ability and technique otherwise we wouldn't have been at United. It wasn't something that was put into us by the coaches, as a group we were always going to be decent players. I was the best player in my age group from Nottingham, Becks was the best in London, Keith Gillespie the best in Northern Ireland and so on.

He benefited from a great scouting system which was put in place by Fergie who had the personal touch to lure us to the club. Eric finished the job and we were more scared of him than the manager himself, he was constantly angry. We could be losing 2-0, bring it back to 2-2 and he'd still have killed us.

He had his favourites and I wasn't really one of them. He got in the head of a lot of the other lads but personally I wasn't scared of him and I don't think he could work me out. He knew that shouting and screaming in my face wouldn't affect me and that probably frustrated him. I sometimes answered back and that could be seen as being unprofessional but I was my own person.

We never fell out but after I left United he never rang me to see how I was doing or took an interest in my career like I know he did with some of the other lads. The biggest compliment that I can give him is that if I was a coach now I'd use some of his methods, but I reckon with how times have changed I'd be running a fine line of getting sacked within a few weeks because you can't shout at young players anymore.

We had a great squad which would have made a decent Premier League side a few years later. Kevin Pilkington was our goalkeeper and a great lad, all goalkeepers are a bit barmy but we always got on well. He sometimes struggled with his kicking but we didn't concede many goals. He went on to have a decent career in the Football League and has only finished playing in the past couple of seasons which is a remarkable achievement when you think about it.

In defence it would be me at right-back with Gary Neville at centre-half. Me and Gary were two completely different people, polar opposites who argued like cat and dog every time we played together. I'd always be dead casual, nip the ball off people's toes and cover his mistakes. He'd want to attack everything and we just didn't respect each other's game. Shouting and bawling wasn't my game at all, I just wanted to play football.

On a personal level we were never really mates and people often say to me that he got my career, but I don't hold any bitterness towards him. As we'll discuss later, life takes you down different paths and whilst I was a better technical player than him at that age, his career and mine turned out to be very different. I enjoy watching him on Sky Sports and he's one of the best pundits around alongside being a successful businessman. There seems to be nothing he can't do, so good luck to him.

We used to call Chris Casper, our other centre-half, 'Turkey Butty' because he was the only one of us who had his foreskin chopped off (sorry Casp). The lads didn't take to him at first because he came from a footballing background, his dad Frank having played for Burnley. We used to take the piss out of him because he was so serious but he mellowed out in the end.

I often played next to him and he used to hate playing with me because I was very off-the-cuff. We were always shouting at each other and slagging each other off on the pitch. Sometimes I would give him a little hospital ball to see how he'd handle it and he'd go mental. He retired quite young because of injury and went on to become the youngest manager in the Football League with Bury.

At left-back was George Switzer, a Salford lad who lived and breathed Manchester United. He was the same build as Patrice Evra and had the sweetest left foot. He could tackle, run and if he'd have had a manager who believed in him or had he played somewhere like Spain, he would have had a decent career but for some reason he was deemed too small and ended up being released. I always remember the look on George's face when they told him he was being let go, he was devastated. He should have been given another year, but they were probably looking at Phil Neville and thought there was no point in keeping him around. It's a brutal business. He went on to play non-league and last I heard he was working as a postman and driving for a living.

I was the ball player in that defence which was one of my strengths as I was brought up to be able to handle it. At a club like United it doesn't matter if you're given it in a situation that's a bit tight, you should know what you're going to do with it before you get it. The best players like Scholesy always think two or three steps ahead and you can't teach that. I could take it in any situation and played with freedom and no fear.

Sometimes in training I would just whip it out to the wing without looking because I knew Ben Thornley would be there. Most of the time though I would just play one or two touch, keeping it simple. In my head I was one of the best players in that side, I could ping a ball with my left or right foot, I had good control and I was a good athlete.

## Paul Gough

*John was like a young Des Walker – quick, very comfortable on the ball and could read the game like an experienced pro. In training matches he'd often play in midfield or up-front and he was comfortable in every position. Not many defenders can score goals yet John had that striker's knack of knowing where the goal is. At that time most English defences were 'strong' and defenders had to be good in the air and win tackles – very few could play out. John could. He would be made for modern day football the way the game has evolved with the likes of Pep.*

*Youth football is so unpredictable and it's almost impossible to say who will become a top player even when players are outstanding at 14 to 18 playing at a top club. Giggsy was an exception – we could all see he was being fast-tracked to the first team as he was a class apart.*

*In the 1992 team, Butty was a stand out player but if you said to the coaches and Fergie back then that four players from the group will go on to be legends and win you the Premier League and Champions League I think they all would have named John in that group, one hundred percent. Keith Gillespie and Ben Thornley might have been in there too - remember Keith made the first team before Becks and was only let go because Keegan insisted on getting him as part of the Andy Cole deal a few years later.*

Right wing would be Becks who could also play in the centre or Keith Gillespie. Keith was a flying winger and a brilliant player, he could be a bit of a maniac when he'd had a drink though. He famously got decked by Alan Shearer when he was at Newcastle and I remember a similar incident occurring with Butty in the showers when he pushed his luck a bit too far. He was as mad as cheese, speaking of which he used to eat blocks of the stuff, something I could never get my head round.

Nicky Butt and Simon Davies usually played centre midfield together. You got what you saw with Butty, he loved the banter but you couldn't mess with him. You always knew he was going to make it and he was one of the coaches' favourites because he was a Manchester lad who was a no-nonsense, tough tackling midfielder, he could play as well.

He was elevated to another level by playing alongside the established players in the first team. He loved the battle, if it was kicking off, he sorted it out. You knew if he was playing we weren't losing the battle in midfield, he did all the graft and was hard as nails. He was a good honest pro and I wish I'd have had his mentality because I'd have gone a lot further.

Simon was a great technical player who played a few games in the first team but was looked upon as having the wrong attitude at the time. I'm surprised that he went into coaching but he knows the game and has done his badges before going on to be successful at City for a good few years.

Ben Thornley was a great winger who suffered a bad injury a couple of years later. He may have struggled to shift Giggs and Lee Sharpe in the first team but unfortunately we'll never know because of what happened. He was the most angry, horrible footballer you'll ever meet on a pitch and always moaned constantly but he was a winner. His pace wasn't electric but he was by no means slow and he could put a great cross in, he used to win us so many games on his own and was a natural on either foot. Off the pitch he's the nicest guy you could ever meet and I still have a lot of time for him now.

Colin McKee was a top striker who scored a lot of goals at that level but he was another one who was given a hard time by the coaches. On his day he was unplayable, very quick and played for the first team before moving back to Scotland to play for Kilmarnock and various others. I've heard he works in the building trade now.

The class clown was Robbie Savage, he was the one who got everyone going and he could laugh at himself. He was an honest player who ran around like a headless chicken but no one worked harder. He didn't weigh anything and played up-front at the time scoring quite a few goals. Like you can see on TV, he's a character and that helped him forge a brilliant career, because he was like that on the pitch. It's a bit of an act though because I know he's a very private family man, quite reserved but it sells and he knows how to get work. He reminds me a bit of Keith Lemon but I still remember him as that innocent young lad with greasy hair who wouldn't take his boxers off when he had a shower…

Others like Raphael Burke, Andy Noone, Joe Roberts, Lenny Taylor and Mark Gordon were all good lads and decent players who played their part. Everyone thinks they've got a chance of making it but the fact is some players are just there to support the stars like Giggsy in a youth team.

We all thought we were going to be millionaires. That's the line the club fed us to get us there and we all bought into it. We didn't even think about contract talks to turn professional at 17 or 18 when we might not be taken on, there's absolutely no loyalty or sentimentality, no goodbyes, players just disappear and you just have to get on with it hoping you won't be next.

## Lenny Taylor – Manchester United Youth Player 1989-92

*United let me go just after the Youth Cup win. I was on the bench for the first leg of the final and got on in the semi-final at Spurs but Gary Neville and John were ahead of me so it was hard work to hold down a regular spot.*

*I had trials with Port Vale, Walsall and then went and played non-league for Solihull Borough – now Solihull Moors. I was about 26 when I stopped playing because things change, you've got to work and survive and football wasn't giving me a proper income so I drifted out of it.*

*Thinking about being part of that team still sends shivers down my spine because we had so much confidence, belief and understanding. It was an absolute pleasure. I'm proud to have been part of that group and I'm proud of the lads who went on to play in the first team and win titles. It was great to see.*

*I lived in digs with John and he was a fun guy to be around. As a player he was silky smooth, strong with excellent feet. You know with Trent Alexander-Arnold people say he's a midfielder playing at right-back? Well, John was doing that 30 years ago…*

In terms of the cup run itself, I don't remember many of the games but I did score against City in one of the earlier rounds at Maine Road where we won 3-1. Any goal against the noisy neighbours is always a good thing! I usually enjoyed playing at Maine Road because it was a big ground with a massive pitch which suited me because it allowed me to ping the ball.

Those were fierce games but we knew a lot of their lads on a personal level because we went to college with them in the week. They weren't great at the time but had Richard Edghill and Steve Lomas in their side. Adie Mike was another who was probably my toughest opponent around that time, he was strong, very direct and could be a bit of a nightmare to play against.

A lot of people had more respect for City then because although they were shit they were a proper club before all the money came in. Their fans then were proper hardcore but when I look at them now and, despite all the success in recent years, they can't even fill out their new ground for big European games. I find that strange.

The crowds and interest was starting to grow but we were conditioned to block it out so it didn't faze us. We'd get decent crowds to watch us play games at the Cliff, easily a couple of thousand sometimes. The only pressure I ever felt was inside my own head – the twitches, nerves and that kind of thing. Having said that I trusted my own ability, every one of us knew we could go out there and rip teams apart and if Giggsy started, the game was effectively over before it began.

We beat Spurs in the semi-finals over two legs, they had a decent team and were probably the favourites. Darren Caskey was being touted as a potential star and they had future England internationals Nick Barmby and Sol Campbell playing for them as well. Barmby was sent off in the first leg at Old Trafford in which Giggsy scored twice and we won 3-0 before finishing the job down in London. It was a great result but it was just another game to us at the time. I know I just turned up and played.

For the final against Crystal Palace I was given the task of marking their best player – George Ndah. He was some player and was being touted as the next big thing at the time. I remember practising against Giggsy in training in the run-up to try and get a handle on what he would be like. Ndah was tall and so fast, but we knew that if we kept him quiet we'd win. The coaches knew that I could handle him but were sure to keep reminding me of the danger he posed: "O'Kane, come on, do you realise how good this guy is! You've got to be on it today!"

As was often the case throughout my career, when I knew I had such an important role in a game or was playing against a top player it spurred me on and more often than not I rose to the challenge.

On the night I snuffed him out. I marked him out of the game and remember daring him to take me on but he couldn't do it. I had intelligence and could read the game. I knew what he was going to do before he received the ball, when to get tight or hang off him. The trick with fast players is to show them inside, "Here's Nicky Butt, all the best mate!"

I think we both relished the battle and respected each other. He was a nice lad and had a decent career with Palace before finishing up at Wolves. They had a good side with Jimmy Glass in net who later scored the famous last minute goal that kept Carlisle United in the Football League.

I'm not saying that was where the game was won and lost but we knew if we stopped Ndah, we had a good chance. I was booked in the first leg at Selhurst Park for a bit of handbags with one of their players, I can't remember exactly what happened but it takes a lot to rile me so he must have done something bad!

We won the second leg at Old Trafford 3-2 to pick up the trophy, Ben Thornley scored a decent goal that's often replayed where he ran in from the left wing and stroked the ball in with his right foot.

Ben Thornley

*We conceded early doors in the second leg which made it close after we'd won 3-1 down there in the first game. My goal came a few minutes before half-time which I think helped to settle everybody down and in the end we won by quite a decent margin, 6-3 on aggregate.*

*John played every game and was exceptionally good all the way through, as most of us were, and we played some difficult games in that cup run.*

*We know that Gary Neville went on to be Manchester United's right-back for the best part of 12-14 years but at the time Gary and Chris Casper were our centre-halves and John had absolutely nailed down the spot on the right-hand side of the defence as his own. I don't think anybody ever challenged him because of his talent and he played a massive part in us winning that trophy and was one of the first names on the team-sheet.*

*It was a great bunch of lads, some of whom went on to have absolutely phenomenal careers and we had great guidance from Eric Harrison. Sir Alex Ferguson also knew what a talented bunch of players that he had and we came from backgrounds where he knew we were going to work hard, there were no bad eggs in there or big-time Charlies and when you've got a great mix of lads who are talented, prepared to listen and put the work in, it was the recipe for success.*

I remember walking round the pitch at the end with Becks celebrating and probably thinking about the night out that we were going to have that night. We had the famous photo on the pitch with the trophy but a lot of it's a blur. We knew the history and what that competition meant to United but beforehand it was just another game to us. It was a big achievement because the last United team to win it before us contained George Best. We won it at a canter, no one really tested us.

We were a special group of players but it wasn't really rocket science. The scouting was top notch and the club had managed to recruit the best player in each area. Fergie had put the scouting network back together. He saw the long-term reward to it when he first took over and the club was going nowhere.

We knew we were good because we used to play against the first team in training and we'd more than hold our own. There's stories of us winning those games, they would have taken it seriously but we were like wasps round them.

I remember the boss and a few of the coaches coming in the dressing room after the cup win to offer congratulations. Some of the first team came in as well but by then the celebrations were in full swing, I don't remember anything organised but we probably ended up going to Royale's, our nightclub of choice at that time.

I didn't really take it all in – I was too young to appreciate it. I just lived in the moment but looking back now it's one of the proudest achievements of my career. Like most of the lads the next logical step for me was to wait for a chance in the first team which would hopefully come sooner rather than later.

## ESTEEMED COMPANY

W̲E SHOULD HAVE WON IT THE following year too but were beaten over two legs in the final by a very good Leeds United side. A lot of teams had grown up whilst we were still a little slight in presence and we got bullied a bit. We'd lost a few players as well because the likes of Giggsy and a couple of others were now too old to play in the competition.

I scored in one of the early rounds against York City in a 5-0 victory at Old Trafford, Paul Scholes laid it on a plate for me and I just had to tap it in. He was a bit of a late developer was Scholesy and never the fittest of lads because he suffered from asthma and was really small. In the early days I thought he had no chance of making it, he honestly didn't seem that good. He was more of a striker then and although he had an eye for goal there were other players ahead of him in the pecking order but then all of a sudden, something just clicked and he was destroying teams on his own. Players develop at different rates, I developed early and he was the opposite. He went from being a little chubby ginger lad to being one of the best players of all time to play for United. With young players, peaking at the right time can be important and he certainly did that. He was a good lad with a great sense of humour as well.

We managed to get past Millwall over two legs in what was a tricky semi-final but the final against Leeds was just too much for us. They had a good core group of players and just came from nowhere, it was like playing against men. I played in the first leg at Old Trafford which we lost 2-0 but missed the second game with an ankle injury, something I often had problems with over the course of my career. I'd go over on my ankles all the time after going up for a ball. Nicky Butt also missed that game and our midfield without him was too lightweight.

The crowds for both games were huge and I think it was shown live on TV given the interest from the previous year – the atmosphere at Elland Road was absolutely toxic. We were battered over the two legs and they beat us fair and square. They had players like Jamie Forrester, who looked like a werewolf, Noel Whelan was a decent player and Mark Tinkler was an absolute beast, he was huge.

From what I remember the gaffer came in and absolutely hammered us all afterwards. He was pissed off that we hadn't turned up, probably because we'd lost to one of the club's main rivals at the time. He ripped us apart, he knew that we were all good players and it would have been to see our reaction. He was testing us.

I found that out for myself when most of the lads, including Becks and Scholesy, were awarded four-year professional contracts. I was only given two years and a lesser signing-on fee because the manager, although acknowledging my undoubted potential, wanted to see more from me.

Fergie was trying to get that bit extra out of me because I think he could see that I was coasting and relying too much on my ability by this point. He wanted me to push myself a bit more rather than just do enough. It was good man management but I took it the wrong way, in my head I was as good as the other lads but I questioned it rather than knuckle down, something that I definitely regret when I look back now. I knew I could train better or run faster than the other lads but something in my make-up stopped me from doing that. I'm not lazy but that's the reputation I got and once I was given that label it was hard to shake off. I've worked 18-hour shifts and I'm probably one of the hardest working ex-footballers you'll ever meet but at the time I just wanted to play football and enjoy myself.

I tell my kids now "hard work beats ability". That maxim forges careers in anything because when that ability fails, what can you fall back on? I relied too much on my talent. I needed hunger and desire to succeed in football and I didn't have enough of it. It just wasn't in my make-up. I had the ability to make it at United but probably lacked some of the mental strength required at the top level.

I could turn it on when I wanted to though, especially if my pride was hurt when I'd run like a maniac if I felt wronged but I often made things look too easy and like I was never exerting myself. Consistency was another issue and I just didn't have enough drive and determination. I always did just enough and you can't do that at a club as big as United.

I've been a coach and seen players like I was at that age and it's about getting inside their heads to get the best out of them. I tested coaches all the time because I'd stick up for myself and they couldn't handle it so I was deemed as having a bad attitude and a chip on my shoulder. I was always taught to speak up and question authority. Having your own mind in an industry like football is dangerous and individual players or characters didn't tend to do well at United around that time, at least not in the young players coming through where you were expected to meet certain standards.

I'd see the lists go up on the wall at the Cliff for who was training with the first team, reserves and so on. I'd notice the likes of Becks would be with the first team and I felt like I was good enough to be training with them but was beginning to fall behind. The likes of Butty, Gary Neville and Keith Gillespie were all given their first team debuts around this time but I was being made to wait for mine or wonder if it would ever come.

I was the sort of player who needed an arm round them and to be trusted but that's not how it was at United, largely due to the fierce competition for places. It all had to come from within yourself and it wasn't the right environment for me.

Fergie moved my mum to Manchester around this time because he thought I was losing my way, I was never a big drinker but liked clothes and looked like a party boy. I was mates with Lee Sharpe who was going that way and the gaffer didn't approve. I moved in with my mum and my step-dad and stayed there until I got my own house.

Like most young people and a lot of the other lads at the club, I was no stranger to Manchester's nightlife and most weeks would follow a similar pattern. We used to go to a seventies night midweek at Discotheque Royales. It would close about midnight and then you'd go home, train and recover the next couple of days then play in your 'A' or 'B' team game on the Saturday morning. We'd watch the first team in the afternoon at Old Trafford and then go out in the evening. It's the best life and I was living it. It was a happy time.

Nowadays players are more or less teetotal, there was no social media then so you could get away with it a bit more but Fergie had his contacts so knew what everyone had been up to anyway. The likes of Neville and Casper never used to come out, it was more the lads from the digs; Colin McKee, Keith Gillespie, Becks every now and then,

Goughy, Sean McAuley, Raphael Burke and Lenny Taylor.

## Paul Gough

*We soon learned that our players pass to get into Old Trafford also offered free entry into Royales nightclub. We didn't have money to throw about like the young players today but we were exposed to the VIP lifestyle, some of the more senior players must have been sorting the bouncers out with tickets because they always let us in.*

*John was always deadly with the women in clubs and it was the same on holiday when we went to places like Cyprus - he had no problem pulling!*

In town, Sharpey would always have a flock of girls around him so the trick was to stand near him and they would be deflected off him and Giggsy. They used to call Sharpey 'The Shark' back then because he was lethal when it came to women. I could hold my own though, I was confident and mature with a bit more hair then.

I remember going out with him one Friday night when he called at the digs because he had no game that weekend. I was due to play in the 'A' team the next morning. I didn't drink but we probably got in quite late and luckily it didn't affect me the next day. We won and I scored as well if I remember rightly before getting called up to the reserves the same afternoon who were going for the league at Old Trafford. I was only 16 or 17 and I only came on for them but that ended up being a long day!

I got this tag of being a big drinker but I wasn't, I remember pouring stuff away because I just couldn't drink it. I used to drink Southern Comfort because it was like drinking pop. I did it purely to fit in and ended up with a reputation for being on drugs as well because everyone knew I was a bit twitchy. I was given the nickname

'Johnny Cocaine' but I never took drugs, mainly because I was too scared of what they would do to me and too strong-minded to be pressured into it. I do remember one occasion where I was actually offered cocaine by another player who had played in the first team at a party but he shall remain nameless.

I enjoyed the social life though and incurred the wrath of the gaffer by being at the infamous house party at Sharpey's. He'd taken Giggsy under his wing around that time and they were both good looking lads of a similar age. People gravitate towards each other and they had a lot in common. Giggsy was beginning to overtake Sharpey in the first team. Lee was starting to lose a bit of his pace – maybe that was down to lifestyle, drinking obviously doesn't help, but that was Sharpey. In fairness to him he was that versatile he could play almost anywhere anyway.

That night there was me, Raphael Burke, Lenny Taylor, Giggsy and maybe Andy Noone and George Switzer as well. We were just invited round before a night out and there were a few girls there, all scantily dressed and getting ready in Sharpey's room. At the time the first team were in a battle for the league title and I think they'd just lost a game.

Fergie got wind that there was something going down at Sharpey's house, how he found out I'll never know but like I say he had his spies everywhere. I remember hearing a knock at the door and excitedly rushing to the top of the stairs thinking it would be more girls. I saw him at the door and froze, I thought I was dreaming. A million thoughts flashed through my mind in just a split second.

I thought about what my mum would think if I was sacked, that he was going to kill me and if there was some way I could get out of it.

My next thought - fucking hide!

I sprinted upstairs, "Lads, the gaffer's downstairs!"

"Haha yeah alright, fuck off."

They just laughed it off and carried on getting ready, doing their hair, ironing their jeans or whatever.

I think I hid either under the bed or in the wardrobe, I wasn't there that long and could hear a kerfuffle going on downstairs.

"YOU LOT GET DOWN HERE NOW!"

He ordered everyone else who was there out of the house and we filed downstairs to face the music. He smacked me round the head as we went into the front room.

"Get in there!"

We sat down.

He went round each one of us. I remember being sat there waiting for my turn worried about what was going to happen but in a weird way part of me enjoyed the drama. I remember his face right in front of mine. The rest of us were then ordered out so he could deal with Giggsy and Sharpey who got the worst of it. They got absolutely blasted.

We went back to the digs and dreaded going into training the next day or the following Monday. Sure enough we were pulled into his office one by one and sat down. He looked at me across his desk and just said, "John, I like you as a person and as a player but if you ever step out of line like that again son, then you're fucking sacked."

And that was it. I walked out, feeling relieved and went out and trained like normal. You move on and that was the great thing about the gaffer, once something had been dealt with he'd forget about it unless it was repeated. I knew he liked me, which is why he ended up keeping me around for so long. That didn't stop me from getting on the wrong side of him on several occasions though.

On another occasion I remember wearing a diamond earring to training one day. Fergie saw it, dragged me into his office, pulled it out, slapped me round the back of the head and told me to "fuck off".

"Get out and don't wear it again!"

We used to sit in the common room area at the Cliff. When he used to come in the mood would change depending on the look on his face - you'd know whether you could either approach him or keep your head down and avoid his glare. He could lose his shit but I wasn't scared of him and he knew that. He used to slap me round the head to get me revved up because he knew that when I was angry or felt that I had been wronged I was a hell of a player and I think he respected me as a person.

By this time the first team were beginning to scale the heights they maintained for the next two decades when they finally won the Premier League title in the spring of 1993 after a 26-year wait. I was at the Sheffield Wednesday game where Steve Bruce scored that late header and Fergie and Brian Kidd celebrated together on the pitch like a pair of maniacs but we missed all the drama because me and Becks had left early to beat the rush and get back to the digs because it looked like we were never going to score and I can remember we celebrated together in the car when news of the goal came through on the radio.

By now I wasn't just a United player but I was also a fan and celebrated every goal as if it was my own. The club had been building for this for the previous two or three years whilst I'd been there and I could sense something was happening. There was so much excitement. I loved the whole build-up of going to training in the morning knowing that there was a game that evening and that I was going to be there watching it. It's an unbelievable feeling as an apprentice because that team was brilliant to watch and you're sat in the stands thinking that one day it could be you out there playing alongside these top players.

Things took a step in the right direction on that front when me and Becks were picked to go on tour with the first team to South Africa in the summer of 1993 just after they'd won the league. I always wonder why it was just us that were picked to go, maybe because Fergie thought we were ready and wanted to take us for the experience or maybe just because we were close at the time and he thought we could support each other through it.

We went out there to play a couple of games and met Nelson Mandela, who had only been released from prison a few years before. I remember it being a long-haul flight and that would have been my first. We flew first class, lying down and watching TV. The pair of us were looking round thinking we'd made it.

I knew very little about the history of South Africa or apartheid but I remember my nana hated Mandela because a lot of white people at the time saw him as a terrorist. I still have a photo of me shaking hands with him and then I remember us doing a question and answer session on stage. It's mad to look back on it now because I'd come from a council estate in Bilborough and here I was meeting this man who is still so famous all around the world even after his death. He did a lot for his country and stood up for what he believed in.

It was my first experience of being around the first team squad but there were other younger players involved which definitely helped. Darren Ferguson went, Giggsy was there too and I remember playing golf or cards with them in the afternoon after we'd finished training. When you're that young you don't really realise the magnitude of what you're doing being on tour in such a historic country with Manchester United, I was just happy to be a part of it. We were probably one of the first sports teams to tour South Africa after apartheid ended, it was ground-breaking.

It was a great experience, Arsenal were over there too. I remember being sat on the bench watching us play them in a packed stadium at Ellis Park in Johannesburg. We lost 2-0 with Ian Wright scoring both their goals. The stadium was huge and just a sea of red from both sets of fans.

I managed to get on the pitch in our next game against Kaiser Chiefs when I came on for Brian McClair in front of another packed crowd of 65,000 people at the FNB stadium. I was on the right wing and remember having a few touches. I just tried to enjoy the moment and not mess up to avoid the wrath of the gaffer. I was probably on for about 20 or 30 minutes to get a taste of first team football.

Every time I played for Fergie I went out there thinking, "I best not fuck up here." I'd keep to what I'd been told which was to pass, move and attack. To an extent any signs of inexperience would be masked by the quality of the more established players around me.

The atmosphere was unreal but when you're playing you don't really hear the noise and it never fazed me. We drew 1-1 and Dion Dublin scored our goal, it was unfortunate that it didn't really work out for him at United with the injury he had and Eric Cantona signing but he was one of the nicest blokes you'll ever meet and always had time for the young players. He had a great touch and awareness and is a rare example of a United player who went on to better things when he left the club.

By the end of the tour I felt I'd done alright and on our

return I began settling into life in the reserves hoping to one day get a chance. I spent a few weeks on loan at a club in Switzerland called Neuchatel Xamax but couldn't play because of an issue with my visa so just ended up training with them.

Reserve team football in those days was a great opportunity to test yourself against experienced first team players and winning the Pontins League, which we did a few times whilst I was at the club, was a big deal. I think it worked better than the current age group system with under-23s because I was playing against men and the standard was much higher, it also means that nowadays the step up into the first team is even more difficult for players coming through whereas we had that grounding.

We had a good side at that level which was a mix of younger players and more senior pros who either couldn't get in the first team or were coming back from injury. The likes of Clayton Blackmore, Brian McClair, Mike Phelan and Bryan Robson were all involved with the reserves on a fairly regular basis around that time so it was a good education for the younger lads like myself, Chris Casper, Pat McGibbon and Ben Thornley among others to be playing alongside them against some top players.

## Pat McGibbon – Manchester United 1992-97

*I played a lot of reserve games with John and you were never scared to give him the ball because you knew he wouldn't be flustered. He was comfortable on it and could play at centre-half or in midfield. He was more of a ball player but he could tackle as well and was competing with Gary Neville for a spot at right-back, it was just a matter of who was going to come through first.*

*We had a really strong second string which was a mixture of first team players and the young lads coming through who didn't* necessarily make it at Manchester United but went on to make good careers for themselves. I was at United for five years and everyone knows that the first team won the league four times over that period but in the reserves we won the league three times as well. It was the same in the 'A' and 'B' teams, there was success fostered throughout the club and competition for places from top to bottom.

If it had been another time in the club's history where they weren't doing as well, then maybe more of us would have got more of a chance in the first team. It's nothing to be embarrassed about not getting the opportunity to play hundreds of games at United, especially in that era.

You had to step up and learn quickly because the standard was decent. I remember playing against Mark Walters who was at Liverpool at the time and had a step-over of death, whatever I did I just couldn't read it and he absolutely rinsed me in a game at Old Trafford.

The games had an edge to them as well, I remember Neil Ruddock breaking Andy Cole's legs in one game at Liverpool. Those games against the Scousers and to a lesser extent City always took on greater meaning no matter what level they were played, as losing was unacceptable.

I felt I'd made the step up to that level without too many problems and with the experiences of South Africa and Switzerland under my belt, but when I was finally given my competitive first team debut it came in slightly less glamorous surroundings.

## WHEN SATURDAY COMES

I T FINALLY HAPPENED ON THE 21ST September 1994. I made my United first team debut as a substitute for Gary Neville of all people in a 2-1 win over Port Vale at Vale Park in a League Cup game. The game is probably better remembered for it being Scholesy's debut as he scored both goals and stole all the headlines.

It's a big moment for anyone and I felt a little bit apprehensive coming on in such a tight game, especially as a defender. I wouldn't say I was an anxious lad but I was twitchy, I was nervous for every game but dealing with everything that was going on in my head often made it much harder. My tics or twitches would get worse in the run up to kick-off and I'd be trying to disguise it or going into the toilet to get a few out and release a bit of it.

It's an impairment and there's no two ways about it, when I got onto the pitch it affected me. It stopped me running like I should have been, imagine playing in a game in front of anything up to 60,000 fans, all with their eyes on you and knowing that they're watching you twitch whilst trying to suppress it and play football at the same time.

I used to flick my right leg up because I needed to have that feeling of my calf straining. It would go in cycles, I'd roll my shoulder or hit myself on the chest and I just couldn't stop myself. People with similar conditions will understand exactly what I mean. The feeling that you need to do a certain movement and won't be satisfied until you do, it's a chemical imbalance in your head.

It's an added pressure on top of everything else that people don't understand. There will be so many people out there who struggle with it but because I was such a strong character, and I had to be, I thought it never really affected me... or so I thought at the time. It's linked to stress and anxiety and I've recently had issues with high blood pressure. I'm a fit lad, I'm healthy but it can cause a build-up of pressure in your head that can be difficult to deal with.

Sat on the subs bench that night at Vale Park, I was excited to have the chance to make my debut but part of me was hoping not to get on as the game wore on because on top of what I had to deal with, in that situation you're sat there not wanting to be the one who makes the mistake that costs the team the game.

It is often quite relaxed on the bench, you've not got the pressure of starting and warming up running down the touchline in front of all the fans is one of the best things you can do. It's not that I wanted to be a substitute in the first place but I often found you enjoy the moment and the atmosphere a bit more. You take more of it in and the ground was packed that night because United were in town.

It was surreal when I got the call to get stripped and go on, loads of stuff went through my mind and I just wanted to keep it simple. The boss would never over-do it with me when it came to instructions, it was just a case of getting out there and not letting yourself down. I definitely didn't want to let him down either.

Once I got on the pitch I just got on with it, I trusted my technique which often got me out of a lot of holes anyway. An early touch settled me down. We scraped through in the end but in the back of my mind I would have been annoyed that I wasn't starting. I always felt like I was one step behind the rest of the lads who went on to become established.

That game ended up being debated in parliament as it was claimed United had put a weakened side out and disrespected the competition which was a little wide of the mark as we won the game and our team contained Keano, Denis Irwin and Brian McClair. Fergie continued to play weakened teams in the League Cup for years afterwards to give young players a chance as United were often concentrating on winning the Premier League and the Champions League, so I think it's fair to say that his approach to the competition was justified.

I started in the return leg at Old Trafford a couple of weeks later and played the whole game as we won 2-0 to progress to the next round with another young side. I think the older players in the first team could see that all these young players were starting to come through and the likes of Robbo and Sharpey probably knew that we were going to take their places in the end.

My next opportunity came in January when I started against Sheffield United in the third round of the FA Cup at Bramall Lane in a more or less full-strength side. I always remember Peter Schmeichel pecking my head and giving me bits of advice before the game. It was a little bit patronising and didn't help my nerves. In fairness he was probably trying to help me but I just wasn't that sort of player. Pete was another winner and I remember whenever I chipped him in training, he'd go mad. Scholesy used to do it to him all the time and get chased across the pitch.

You block a lot of stuff out from keepers because to be honest a lot of them are absolutely mental. I know a lot of the first team didn't really get Peter's personality but maybe it was just down to cultural differences. He was a world-class goalkeeper though and his reaction saves were something else. He could kick and throw a ball without any problems too.

I always felt that whenever I came into the squad, my perceived fragile mentality meant that a lot of the senior players would come up and try to reassure me. I get what they were trying to do but I just wanted to be left alone to get my head in the right place to go out and play with my tics under control. I got nicknamed 'The Spaceman' because I sometimes seemed a bit detached or like I was on my own planet. Everyone has their own way of dealing with the nerves and the pressure and with me being on the spectrum my brain was wired up differently to everyone else's.

The best piece of advice that day came from one of the quieter players in the dressing room – as we were heading out Eric Cantona just looked at me and said, "Don't be like everyone else."

It was one of my most enjoyable games for United and they ended up making it into a film, *When Saturday Comes* with Sean Bean. It was really windy and there were crisp packets and other rubbish flying everywhere. It was cold, raining and the pitch was awful but I remember feeling really comfortable for the hour or so that I played and then I was brought off!

I'd started getting a bit giddy bombing forward. I was living in the moment and it was one of those games where I just felt free. I was just used to attacking and probably lost a bit of discipline so the gaffer brought me off for Lee Sharpe after just over an hour because it was still 0-0. I think he was worried about me overlapping and leaving space for them to hit us on the break.

I was a bit gutted but we won it late on when Sparky put us ahead before Cantona scored a superb chip over the keeper a couple of minutes later. I remember Fergie jumping into my arms and I caught him. I've still got the picture and look a little embarrassed in it. It was a tough game and they fought hard after having a man sent off but we battled through it and outclassed them in the end because we had better players.

I was starting to get a look-in with the first team and would make the squad from time to time or travel as cover. I was in the party that travelled to Gothenburg for a Champions League game. The gaffer took a few of the younger lads which was a good experience even though I didn't make the bench. I think that was the game that put Jesper Blomqvist on the club's radar because I remember being sat in the stands whilst he ran us ragged. He was ridiculous.

Even getting called to train with them was a step up, Brian Kidd was a great coach. Until recently he was in the background at City and it's not surprising how well they've done over the last ten years with his knowledge and experience of the game. His training sessions were way beyond anything that I'd experienced before. It was elite level and would include passing sequences and patterns of play, I'd not done training like that before. I wasn't really close to him and he had his favourites which were usually the local Manchester lads but he was one of the best coaches that I ever worked with. He was second to none and the gaffer always had a good number two.

I enjoyed being around the first team and although I was never really a permanent fixture in their dressing room I got on well with a lot of the lads. They were all decent and people always say to me how lucky I am to have been able to play alongside all those great players but it's not something I ever really think about too much. At the end of the day they were just colleagues who were very good at what they did and are put on a pedestal by the fans. Footballers aren't any better than the average person just because of what they do for a living. They have their flaws just as normal people do, no one's perfect at the end of the day and trust me it's not the same from the inside looking out of that bubble as it is when you're a fan as I am now.

Two weeks after the Sheffield United game, Cantona jumped into the crowd at Crystal Palace and booted that fan – the infamous kung-fu kick. Eric was a genius but often they have a flipside like George Best and Gazza did. He was given a nine-month ban and it was one of those times around the club where we kept our heads down because we didn't want to get in the way of the boss or Eric whilst they were both dealing with the implications of the situation.

I played in some of the behind closed doors matches that the club organised for him to keep him interested until the FA put a stop to that as well. Fergie would have done everything to help him and keep him on side and it was justified because he was his best signing. He was the cherry on the cake. Eric was temperamental and you never knew what you were going to get from him. He'd never settled before he came to United or had a manager who believed in him and people underestimate how important that is. He chose the right person at the right time in Fergie because if the boss believed in you, then he would stick by you.

Eric's influence had changed the culture of the club; before he arrived we'd be eating sausage, chips and gravy for dinner thinking it was great but that all changed soon after he came in. The theory was that we'd run off the mashed potato, Yorkshire puddings and custard and sponge for afters – there just wasn't the same knowledge about diet in English football that exists today. He had a more continental outlook on food and they soon introduced pasta after that to bring us a little bit more in line with what they were doing in other countries.

That said, it didn't change overnight and in the morning before training we used to go for a cup of tea and a bacon sarnie but Eric would already be outside, kicking balls up in the air and controlling them. He had such a good first touch. So after a while everyone was out on the pitch an hour before we were due to start.

As a person he had that aura about him and I loved him. He wasn't an ordinary human being, look at the stuff he's come out and said, he makes you think. He didn't say much but if he looked at you and smiled you were on cloud nine. He was never a sheep or one to follow the crowd and it was one of the highlights of my career to have had the pleasure to share a pitch with him a couple of times for the first team.

It was the same when he shocked everybody and quit the game at the age of 30 a couple of years later. He went out on his own terms and could easily have had another three or four years but he knew the time was right for him to finish. They say there's a fine line between greatness and madness...

I was a regular for the reserves by this point and now felt established at that level. I got on well with Jim Ryan the coach but always felt that he was having a go at me. He used to give me a lift from the Cliff to Littleton Road and I remember one day confronting him about it in the car. He just said, "The time I stop going on at you John, then you'll know you're finished." It was a lightbulb moment for me and I tell my kids now, if a coach or boss is having a go, it means that they see something they're trying to bring out which is what Jim was trying to do. He always used to be on at me and I was probably too immature to see the bigger picture, I just thought he was coming at me all the time and the world was against me.

I felt hard done by in terms of how I was used at that level and by the likes of Eric Harrison in the youth sides, because I was so versatile I was often moved around to where I was needed instead of being allowed to settle and grow into one position, like Gary Neville and Becks who were starting to get a run of games in the first team and if I had been allowed to do that, I would probably have had a better career.

I used to turn up for games with no idea of where I'd be playing that day and it didn't help me settle or gain any sort of momentum. I was almost taken advantage of in that regard. When I came to United I was a centre-half, I was tall when I was younger but then I levelled out and because I could play I got moved out to right-back. From centre-half I could read the game and I loved playing there but because I wasn't the most vocal and maybe lacked a couple of inches in height I didn't get the chance to really play in my preferred position.

## Ben Thornley

*Once Gary Neville got in the first team and dislodged Paul Parker at right-back he made that position his own for a long time and you couldn't see anyone getting past him. I think when John came to the club he saw himself as a centre-half but sometimes things change. It happened to me as well, when I played for Salford Boys I played centre midfield with Nicky Butt but United converted me to a winger because I had a bit of pace and wanted to go past players. It didn't really bother me because I enjoyed playing there and it was a similar situation with John, but I think although he was an exceptionally good right-back and made a good career there, centre-half was where he always saw himself and he was a bit despondent that he was never given the chance to play there. He was definitely at the right club but I think he felt he never got a fair crack of the whip by playing in his preferred position.*

Around that time I remember the likes of Scholesy, Butty and Becks being worried about their chances of becoming established in the first team. My attitude was that if it was going to happen it would happen. Becks ended up going out on loan to Preston, Keith Gillespie had gone to Newcastle permanently and Butty was disillusioned but made the step up eventually.

I went on loan to Wimbledon that summer to play in the early rounds of the old Intertoto Cup. Graeme Tomlinson and Michael Appleton were sent from United as well. They were both good lads and Graeme was one of my best mates at United, he was a good strong player who was bought from Bradford but got a bad injury and never recovered. He used to be a good DJ and I think that's what he went on to do in the end but I ended up losing touch with him after we both left the club.

It was like a reserve or youth squad that was thrown together for the competition. Everyone remembers the Wimbledon side of that time as 'The Crazy Gang' with hard men like Vinnie Jones, Dennis Wise and John Fashanu but there were no first team players involved, although Jason Euell did play but he was still quite young at the time. I'm not sure if the senior players just didn't fancy coming back off holiday early or there was another reason why we all had to be drafted in to help them out.

I played three games, losing 4-0 against Bursapor of Turkey and drawing with Beitar Jerusalem as well as a memorable trip to Slovakia for another draw with FC Kosice. I remember buying a bottle of champagne for a quid! We didn't take it too seriously and I think we actually went out the night before the game.

The three of us had a good time and stayed in Wimbledon while the tennis was on, it was like an all-expenses paid holiday. It was a posh area and we met up with Dean Richards who played for Wolves and Spurs and is sadly no longer with us. He was Graeme Tomlinson's best mate and we went to Ministry of Sound in London, we were just young lads enjoying life.

It was a nice break from the routine at United. At the time they were homing in on Gary Neville as the right-back for the future and if I was to be sent out on loan it was because I was expendable. The door to the first team was closing but maybe there was still time to turn it around and stake a claim.

## SLIDING DOORS

THE FIRST DAY OF THE SEASON IS A great time to be a footballer. You're usually optimistic for the campaign ahead and glad to see the back of pre-season and the endless running that comes with it, especially in those days.

Nowadays players have their own training programmes before actual official pre-season begins but in those days we used to go to Ayia Napa and party until 6am before spending the day asleep on the beach. I was naturally fit anyway but I was a big lad with a playing weight of twelve stone so struggled a bit on the dreaded long distance runs because of my physique. I hated them more than anything in the world but I used to blitz the short sprints and ball work because that's what I was built for.

Again, the laid-back or lazy tag would come into play from the coaches who'd expect me to be up at the front with the likes of Becks and Savage who both weighed about five stone and could run all day. It's a bit like telling Usain Bolt to run a marathon, although I don't claim to be anywhere near as fast as him. I can still hear Eric Harrison now, "O'Kane, get to the front! Stop being lazy!"

So many players get given a label early on that stays with them and honestly I don't really want to bring this into it but it's worse if you're black or mixed-race. For some reason it's easier to get branded as having a bad attitude or a chip on your shoulder. Andy Cole was one; he was a brilliant, funny guy who was very down to earth but got labelled by the media and people in the game as arrogant and moody. I might have had quite a relaxed running style but I was actually busting a gut. Once I had been tagged with that label it was impossible to shake off. Keep throwing enough shit at a wall and some of it will stick and it's something that continued throughout my career.

I'd played a few times in pre-season friendlies after returning from Wimbledon against Shelbourne, East Fife and Oldham. Those games were just about getting us fit and I was just pleased to be in and around the squad. I was also responsible for shaving Sharpey's head on the trip to Scotland to give him the bald look he sported around that time. That's my main memory - my barbering skills!

That summer was a busy one at the club as Fergie sold Sparky, Incey and Kanchelskis. There was uproar when they weren't replaced but within the club there was a sense that the manager was clearing the way for some of the younger lads to progress. He saw the bigger picture and realised he had to trim the squad.

Sparky was one of my favourite players to watch in the way that he played every week. The way he held up the ball and how he'd battle with defenders, in a way I was jealous of the nastiness that he had because my own game lacked it. Incey was a typical cockney, with an air of arrogance about him but we always got on. He was brash and his car sported a number plate that read 'Guvnor' which wouldn't have gone down well with the manager who probably saw Scholes and Butt coming through alongside Roy Keane and thought he had to go.

I remember watching Andrei's first game at Old Trafford against Notts County, we knew he was fast because we'd seen him in training but that night he was ridiculous and I almost couldn't believe my eyes. He didn't speak much

English and had his own interpreter. That didn't stop him being a bit of an extrovert who had a lot of confidence in himself and he was an absolute madman when it came to drinking. I loved watching him play and he was a proper old-fashioned winger but Fergie knew that Becks was coming through so it was time for him to move on as well.

I was named on the bench for the opening day game against Aston Villa at Villa Park in a young squad that also contained the Nevilles, Butty, Scholesy and Becks. Eric was still banned at the time and there would have been a couple of injuries.

From a team point of view, it was a disaster because we were 3-0 down at half-time. In situations like that Fergie would have either gone ballistic at half-time or he could be very calm and just tell us to go out and win the second half. I came on for Gary Pallister after about an hour and Becks scored a late consolation from about 25 yards. It was his first Premier League goal and I remember running over to celebrate with him.

It was a very sunny day and Villa Park was one of the best grounds I played at with a great atmosphere. They were blitzing us and I remember slide tackling Dwight Yorke as last man in defence when they broke away from one of our corners to save a goal. I had a really good game and enjoyed being on the pitch. I didn't give the ball away but remember being told off afterwards for doing Cruyff turns and backheels. There was no pressure on me coming on though and I felt able to express myself. It was another game where I felt free and I didn't get that with football a lot.

Obviously we were disappointed with the result and knew that Fergie wouldn't be happy but secretly I came off buzzing. I knew I'd played well and the adrenaline or high

I got from knowing that was the best feeling in the world. It's difficult to replicate again in life once you've finished playing. It's indescribable and coming back on the coach that day I knew I hadn't done my future first team chances any harm. I know Becks would have been feeling the same way as well.

That game has now become more memorable for Alan Hansen's 'You can't win anything with kids' comment on *Match of the Day* that night. In fairness to him he's a legend for what he did in the game and we were probably sat there after being battered 3-1 thinking he was right. I wouldn't have taken too much notice anyway but the comment would have got the first teamers' and the manager's backs up.

The reason that I didn't play a part in making him eat his words by the end of the season probably lies with my next first team appearance a few weeks later. I made my European debut against Rotor Volgograd at Old Trafford and was subbed after just 26 minutes...

Whenever I was in the squad we'd never find out the team until we met up for the pre-match meal. The gaffer unveiled the flip chart like he always did and the words jumped off the page:

'O'KANE – RIGHT-BACK'

Straight away it hit me, the nerves kicked in because I realised that instead of watching this game as I'd expected, I was now going to be playing in it. The need to prepare yourself physically and mentally becomes paramount. At that point it was probably the biggest game of my career so far, a European game under the lights at Old Trafford. We were getting changed to go out and warm up, I'd been playing left-back for the reserves all season and felt settled there. It sounds stupid but I couldn't get it out of my head that I was going to screw up if I played on the opposite side.

A battle was raging in my head with self-doubt thrown in on top of the usual twitches that I had to contend with and was trying to suppress. Not to mention the nerves that were par for the course anyway. As we left the dressing room to warm up I doubled back and followed the gaffer down the corridor to his office. I knocked on...

"Gaffer, I've been playing left-back all season in the reserves and I feel comfortable there. I was wondering could I not play on the other side?"

He stared at me...

"Ok John, no problem. I'll swap you with Phil Neville."

He knew me as a person and probably respected that I had the balls to go and talk to him about how I felt. I look back on it now and wonder what the hell I was doing questioning the formation or where I was playing just before kick-off but in my head at the time I was convinced I would do a better job for him on the left-hand side.

As luck would have it their right winger, who went by the name of Valery Yesipov, was their best player and we were 2-0 down within 25 minutes. I remember one run he made where he knocked it past me and I was quick but I just couldn't get near him. It was like marking Kanchelskis again and he got round me a couple of times.

It shook me and I remember playing a negative pass where I just played the ball back to Steve Bruce to take the safe option rather than looking forward. Fergie knew that wasn't like me and I could hear him going mental on the sidelines. It was a cop out and I felt that I didn't want it.

My legs seized up and it felt like I was having an out-of-body experience. It was like it was happening to another person. Looking back it was probably the pressure and I couldn't handle it on the night. Sometimes the crowd hits you and when the music comes on before the game you look around and think, 'What the fuck am I doing here?'

I saw the fourth official's board go up after nearly half an hour to indicate a substitution and realised it was me coming off. I wanted the ground to swallow me up. I slunk off with my head down and took my seat on the bench. I was gutted. The game was televised so I was ashamed and embarrassed because my friends and family would have been watching. Again, I wondered what my mum would think.

I was still a fan so watching the rest of that game from the bench I was willing the lads on and resisting the urge to feel sorry for myself. You just don't want it to be seen as your fault that we lost. The lads got it back to 2-2 with Scholesy scoring before Peter Schmeichel scored his famous goal from a corner which gave the game another significance rather than the one where I was subbed after less than half an hour. I was still gutted though.

It was a real *Sliding Doors* moment when I look back at it. If I hadn't swapped positions with Phil Neville, who knows where my career could have gone or what would have happened with his but life takes you down different paths. It was probably the worst footballing decision I made and one of the few times that I regret speaking up.

Out of the seven competitive games I played in the first team, it's probably the one that United fans remember me for. I've beaten myself up about it for more than 25 years, but to be honest and I've never really said this before I actually don't think I played that badly. It's just the guy I was playing against was lightning quick, I wasn't having any impact on the game and had made a negative pass. We were two goals down so the manager had to make a tactical change to try and save the game. I was a negative player for him that night so he brought on Scholesy to give us more options going forward.

I knew that my United first team career was probably over at that point though because I couldn't step up in a game of that size. Even though it was a tactical decision to bring me off, something wasn't right and I didn't feel comfortable.

I had the talent to play at the top level and if it was down to that alone I would have played for England. The thing I didn't have was the mentality, which is if anything more important and it just wasn't in my make-up. I was impaired mentally with my tics and being on the spectrum which isn't an excuse, but it didn't help by any means.

At the time, I was probably having a mini breakdown but the twitching and fighting to suppress it had given me such a strong exterior, like an armour. I was so strong mentally to be able to cope with that but I'd also been scarred by it. I was probably depressed but there wasn't the same awareness around mental health then so I just had to get on with it. United was an old school environment and although the club achieved great success at that time, only the toughest survived.

I can guarantee my performance would have been spoken about among the coaches in the days and weeks after the Rotor game. At every club there is a plan for every player and what they're capable of so they'd be thinking they'd found my limit, "John's just not got it has he? He isn't up to it."

I don't remember having a conversation with Fergie about it but to be fair he was probably sick of the sight of me because I'd go into his office and talk to him about anything. He was like a father figure. He was ruthless when he needed to be but if you had any problems he would listen and help sort them out. I used to have conversations with him when I became disillusioned at not being involved in the first team saying that I wanted to leave or give up football altogether.

He'd look at me across his desk and say, "John you're a player, you're a Manchester United player and you should be my right-back, but there's something in your head that you've got to work out."

I'd leave his office still none the wiser as to how to do that. I respected him though and he was the first male figure in my life that I felt that for. He knew every player at that club from the first team right down to the schoolboys who came and trained twice a week. His attention to detail and work rate was frightening.

The only other time I got on the pitch for the first team that season was when I was part of a squad sent to play in Paul McStay's testimonial game at Celtic Park on a freezing December night just before Christmas. I spent the rest of the season playing for the reserves whilst the likes of Becks, Gary Neville, Scholesy and Butty went on to another level and achieved a double with the first team. I must have gone to the FA Cup final at Wembley where Cantona scored that late winner against Liverpool because attendance was compulsory but I have absolutely no recollection of it.

I was gutted because I knew I was good enough and should have been involved. It was one of the greatest times in the history of Manchester United and I was so close to being a part of it. It's partly my fault as well because I didn't have the drive or desire to look like I wanted it. I was too easy-going and nothing fazed me. I had this demeanour which made it look like I wasn't bothered but deep down it hurt me and I knew that I hadn't worked hard enough.

I was like two people. One side of me didn't care or pretended it didn't whilst the other was telling me to shape up and try harder. They were wrestling in my head, the guy who doesn't want to conform or respect authority which was about 70% and the other which made up about 30% who had a love of football I'd first discovered playing on the streets of Nottingham and wanted to do as well as possible. I should be studied because in the end the 70% side won and destroyed the other side and that's what would eventually take me out of the game.

I always felt that the world owed me a living and I realise now that was wrong. I thought somebody owed me something and I didn't go and get it like Gary Neville did. He'd established himself in the first team by this point and although we played in the same position I never saw him as a rival because to be honest my biggest rival was myself. I still cheered him on as a fan and enjoyed watching the first team even though I knew it could have been me on the pitch rather than sat in the stands. He loved the club and there was no bitterness there at all. I still get ribbed about it from my mates now but that's just life. I didn't want it or care enough at the time.

Gary worked hard to make himself a better player and he went on to become one of the best right-backs in the world. He was lucky to have had Becks playing in front of him but sometimes you need a bit of good fortune to get your career off the ground. He had the drive and desire to go and be successful which ultimately I lacked.

I felt hard done by when I wasn't in the first team or training with them, it's a stupid mentality. Absolutely criminal. I distinctly remember one training session when most of the lads in the reserves were sent over to train with the first team and I was left behind. I was so pissed off, we were playing five-a-side and I just went in goal and put my hands on the crossbar to pretty much lean on the small goal and just stood there.

I'm determined to make sure my kids don't repeat the same mistakes and I've drummed it into them that they need to work hard. I'm the perfect example for them because that's the opposite of what I did. You learn from experience and I've always made sure I worked hard in jobs I've had since leaving football.

A lot of it stems from my upbringing and having everything handed to me on a plate. My mum always drummed into me that I was the best and gave me the impression that I was never wrong. She was a great mum who gave me everything and that was the point. I was spoilt in a way and had no dad to keep me in check and tell me to pull my socks up and try harder like Neville did. Once it's part of your personality it's hard to break and I only did that when I eventually quit the game.

In my mind at the time, I was probably too comfortable. I might get into the first team now and then but I developed this attitude that football was just my job and I loved the life away from it. I was John who played football for Manchester United, just not really in the first team. There was an acceptance from me that I was at the biggest club in the world, earning a living and not really doing too badly for someone who wasn't that bothered about the game.

I enjoyed socialising, I liked girls and just wanted to enjoy life. I was enjoying the moment and wasn't 100% focused on football. The nineties were a great time to be young and Manchester was the place to be, it was exploding. I was lost in the social scene which kind of engulfed me. If my football career had ended the following day I would have just shrugged my shoulders and asked "what next?".

I was still a decent player though and I knew that if I was to have any sort of future in the game, I needed to get out and play.

# MOVER AND SHAKER

I T WASN'T COMPLETELY OVER FOR ME as a first team player at United. An injury crisis in November 1996 meant I started two games within the space of a week; away at Middlesbrough in the Premier League and at Filbert Street against Leicester City in the League Cup.

I played left-back at the Riverside and Michael Clegg made his debut on the opposite flank, Ben Thornley also started so there were quite a few regular first teamers missing. We'd never find out the team until the pre-match meal but you'd often be looking round at who was in the squad and with the lads who travelled that day I fancied my chances of starting.

There were still enough experienced heads though: Schmeichel, Cantona, David May and Roy Keane all started to set the standard for the lads coming into the team. I liked Keano, on the pitch he played the part of the hard man and motivator and he trained like an animal because he was just a complete winner. You can see that side of him in his punditry on TV with his brutal, cutting comments – people say he's a dinosaur in his way of thinking but that way got results for him.

Away from football he was loyal to his team-mates, I remember being on a couple of nights out with him and he wasn't particularly keen on mixing with the fans. He just wasn't that sort of guy but he had a good sense of humour and could make you laugh. He was decent once you got to know him.

Despite what perceptions people might have had of me, I always made sure that I prepared properly for every game by going to bed early the night before, eating the right food and getting myself focussed. I'd always try and be quite jovial in the dressing room beforehand, trying not to take things too seriously. You don't really notice what everyone else is doing because you're in your own little bubble but it was usually quite relaxed, there would be players reading the paper or watching TV, there was no ghetto blaster or anything like that.

I'd get my strappings done, then have a massage and go out to warm up. I'd come back in and the gaffer would give his team talk which was usually pretty long and detailed. Then after that it was up to me and I just wanted to get out onto the pitch and get on with it.

Boro were a good side at the time under Bryan Robson with some great players and I remember Juninho and Fabrizio Ravanelli running at me. They were a handful to deal with and I remember Ravanelli pinning me to try and get a shot away at goal. We took the lead twice through Roy Keane and David May but I conceded an indirect free-kick from which Scholesy handballed so they equalised with a late penalty from Craig Hignett and it finished 2-2.

My mate Robbo came to watch me play in the Leicester game a few days later. He was a tough tackling midfielder and he knew that wasn't my style but I remember him telling me afterwards that I should have absolutely nailed Emile Heskey at one point when we were both going for the ball. He was running down the wing and all I had to do was slide in and take him out but I missed it completely and he got past me. Steve had a right go at me about it afterwards.

## Steve Robinson

*I went that night with my dad. I think it was Emile Heskey who overran the ball and it was a great opportunity for John to time a tackle and take the ball and the man. It was the perfect chance for a defender to hit a forward in the legal sense of the game.*

*Heskey knew he wasn't going to get this ball and it was probably about 80/20 in John's favour but instead of going in for the tackle he's waited a bit and tried to slide to scoop the ball back into play. He's over-thought it and Heskey ended up flicking the ball over John, running down the line and putting a cross in.*

*It was almost like he was thinking that taking the man and ball was too easy for him. All the other top defenders would have done that but not John. Sometimes it was like he had too much talent and not enough of the nuts and bolts.*

Filbert Street was packed that night and it was a great atmosphere. It was a second-string side with a lot of young players in the squad and we got bullied, losing 2-0 with Heskey and Steve Claridge scoring for them. I was brought off after just over an hour and I didn't know it at the time but that would be my last action as a United first team player.

The writing was on the wall though, when the first team players that were missing were back to full fitness I was back in the reserves. I needed to get out so when the chance came to go to Bury on loan to get some more first team experience I jumped at it. They were in the old Division Two (third tier) and were a tough side with some good players.

The club itself was very down to earth with no frills and the facilities were basic but I loved it. People probably thought that with my make-up that I would turn my nose up at it or go missing but in actual fact it suited me.

The contrast with United was massive. The changing rooms were scruffy, cold and wet but I enjoyed it more because of that. I was already familiar with playing at Gigg Lane for United reserves so it wasn't much of a change in that respect and I lived in Radcliffe at the time which was a five-minute drive away from the ground so the whole arrangement was ideal.

The gaffer, Stan Ternent, was an old school manager but he knew how to man-manage me. He had this energy and enthusiasm for me and I just fed off it. I needed a manager to converse and engage with and he did just that. He treated me with respect and he trusted me, our relationship was a successful one because I played in what was already a good team and we ended up winning the league that season.

He was as tough as Fergie and could give out some right rollickings but I took it because I respected him. I remember one game when he went mental at half-time and ripped into players because we were getting bullied and that didn't happen with that team. I also got on very well with his assistant Sam Ellis who was in the mould of Eric Harrison but got me as a player.

They gave me an almost free role where I'd operate as kind of a wing-back which gave me licence to get forward because they had players who could defend. I was an extra attacking option for them and I just went out every week and played my game.

## Stan Ternent – Bury manager 1995-98

*John O'Kane was a fantastic footballer with mountains of natural ability. I needed someone who could play at left-back and John had come through at Manchester United with a good crop of young players playing regularly in that position. He was a very* talented lad so I rang Alex Ferguson to ask if I could take him on loan and he agreed.

Jill Neville, Gary and Phil's mum, was my PA and I knew all about United through their dad Neville. Alex would often help me out with players, I got David Johnson from him and he was good to me on many occasions. We would go and play practice games at the Cliff if one of their players was suspended or coming back from injury to try and return the favour, so we had a good relationship.

Youngsters at a club as big as United are the cream of the cream and John had all the attributes. He was top drawer. You don't go there as a young player if you're not at that level so we knew what we were getting. He was quick and comfortable playing on either side. He was very versatile and could play in a number of positions across the defence and midfield if I needed him to without any problems.

What I saw in John O'Kane was a fantastic athlete and a very good technical player with a God-given gift but as a person he was very laid-back – horizontal sometimes. I think that frustrated a lot of people who may have misinterpreted it that he didn't care enough when in fact the exact opposite was true. You just needed to know the boy and understand him. He was maybe a bit misunderstood at times.

He was a quiet lad and not the type of player you could motivate by giving him a hard time. You needed to talk to him and encourage him. He thrived off having somebody believing in him and showing a bit of confidence. You just needed to give him the right platform to perform.

We had a great team at Bury with many highlights in the time I was there including getting to Wembley, getting promoted twice and beating Manchester City at Maine Road so it was a really good side which John came and played in.

He played regularly during the time he was with us. We ended up winning the league to go up to the Championship and John played a very big part in that with some big performances. We wanted to keep him but Alex needed him back towards the end of the season as cover for the first team because United were pushing for the Premiership.

He did play a few games in United's first team and could have gone all the way but I think Alex got frustrated because he maybe wanted a bit more from him. I don't think John realised how talented a player he was because playing football came naturally to him.

In the end John didn't really fulfil his potential in the game which was a shame but when you're playing at the highest level for the likes of Manchester United it ain't easy. He's a good lad who always did really well for me and was often misunderstood. I hold him in high regard and wish him all the very best.

I made my debut in a home game against Bristol Rovers and it went well, I scored the winner! It was my first professional goal but I didn't actually see it go in. The ball was slightly behind me and I just swung my leg on the volley and by the time I hit the floor it was in the back of the net. It was a great moment and meant the supporters took to me straight away. They were real fans who lived and breathed their club and I loved the whole set-up.

When you go out on loan to a club from United there's often a little bit more pressure on you because you need to convince the fans that you're up for it and actually want to be playing for their club. You're playing against men but you're also treated like one, unlike the lifestyle I was used to where everything was done for you.

We had a good side with some great players, many of whom went on to even bigger things. Dean Kiely was the best goalkeeper in the division by a mile and he went on to play in the Premier League with Charlton Athletic. There was also Mike Jackson, Chris Lucketti, Lenny Johnrose, Paul Butler and David Johnson who'd been a promising young player at United a few seasons earlier until he suffered a bad knee injury. David Pugh was another good player, we had some great characters and played against some good sides in decent stadiums. That team didn't mess about and was similar to a Sam Allardyce sort of team in the way it played; very direct and no-nonsense.

I scored a good goal at Preston from a corner routine that we'd worked on in training. We'd play it short and then float it into the edge of the box, pass it to me and I curled it into the top bin. David Moyes also scored in that game which we lost 3-1 at Deepdale but we didn't lose many.

I loved being part of a first team set-up and I was playing well in a team that was successful. Gigg Lane was packed for most of our games. It was one of the most successful times in Bury's history and it was great to be a part of it and help them get promoted.

I went on their end of season trip to Magaluf which was absolute filth - pure drinking and I think even the chairman was out there to celebrate the club's promotion. It was a big piss up and I was still a bit of a lightweight. The players there saw me as a bit of a posh kid because I was quite preened whereas they were all rough and ready. I remember us all sitting round a table playing drinking games with loads of girls and it was brilliant.

I shared a room with a lad called Tony Rigby who was short and dumpy but a fan's favourite as he was a decent little playmaker who was technically brilliant. Certain players at certain clubs are the centre of the dressing room and he was exactly that at Bury.

He was probably one of the funniest lads I've ever met

and he was absolutely lethal with women. He had the gift of the gab and took me under his wing a little bit. I actually bumped into him a while ago on a night out and he was wearing a big agent's coat and fake tan. He nudged me in the back and I thought I was being started on at first! But it was great to see him and have a catch-up after so many years. He was a really nice lad.

I know Stan tried to sign me permanently at the end of the season and I wanted to go but United refused unless Bury met their valuation which obviously they couldn't afford. I believe United wanted £500,000 for me which in those days was a lot of money for a reserve team player so I was priced out of it and was brought back either as cover for the first team or to make up the numbers in the reserves. It was ruthless in a way as United were looking after themselves and not really considering my best interests as a player, it's tough because those type of decisions can shape a player's career.

Bury was a fantastic club to be a part of and I was gutted when I saw them go through the problems they had which culminated in them being kicked out of the Football League. It's not nice to see such a historic club going out of business just because of the greed and mismanagement of the people running it behind the scenes but there's not a lot you can do as a fan.

It's the supporters who have suffered the most because they've got no football to go and watch each week now, which is almost unthinkable. They live for their weekends and live and breathe the club and now it's just gone. Hopefully they can come back in time. I lived in Bury and it's a small town with the football club at its heart so it's a massive loss for the local community too.

At that stage I knew my time at United was up and

wanted to leave permanently but it wasn't happening so I went out on loan again, this time to Bradford City where Chris Kamara was manager. It was a decent size club with a nice ground in Valley Parade which had been more or less rebuilt following the Bradford stadium fire in the eighties and attracted a decent amount of fans, I remember it being jam-packed and a tremendous atmosphere. They were always right behind us and it felt like there was a bit more pressure because of that.

Again the fans took to me because I did pretty well in the handful of games that I played for them, winning man of the match a couple of times if I remember rightly. I was used in quite a few different positions but I didn't mind. I was sent off for a second bookable offence in a home game against Sheffield United and I also played in a 1-0 defeat to Manchester City at Maine Road where we conceded a last-minute winner.

I got on really well with Chris and enjoyed playing for him. He was as mad as a hatter but at the same time he was a winner. In his playing days he'd been a no-nonsense centre-half and he was very good tactically and as a man-manager as well. He wasn't scared to have a joke with you either, Paul Jewell, his assistant, was the more serious one.

Chris rated me and saw me as a special player who he gave a lot of freedom. Like Stan, he understood my personality and that I wasn't a normal pro. I was sent out to go and play. People probably see him on Sky Sports and think that he's a bit daft but he knows his football. He was the sort of manager who kept me on my toes and you never knew what was going to happen on any given day. You could turn up one morning to training and we could be doing long distance runs, shape work or going paint-balling. It was that off-the-cuff.

They had a good squad and would go on to win promotion to the Premier League within a couple of seasons. Former United keeper Gary Walsh had of course previously been understudy to Peter Schmeichel, former Manchester City winger Peter Beagrie was there, Wayne Jacobs was a very good left-back and I used to room with Jamie Lawrence on away trips who wrote his own book *From Prison to the Premiership.* Darren Moore played in defence, he was a big tough lad but such a nice guy, a gentle giant and a top-drawer professional. Of course he later went into management, at first with West Brom, then Doncaster and at the time of writing he is in charge of Sheffield Wednesday.

Chris wanted to sign me and I remember being in the chairman's office with him telling me they wanted to buy me but couldn't afford it. It was a similar situation to what had happened at Bury. I know he has mentioned it before on his chat shows on Sky that I was a good player and one who got away but Fergie just wouldn't let me go.

So it was back to United again and reserve team football which by that stage was horrible. It was like I'd seen the light whilst being out on loan but kept being dragged back and couldn't get out. I was at United four years too long when I think about it and I became institutionalised, just going through the motions and almost coasting. You're just going through the same repetitive routine and to break it, you've got to wake up but at the same time I had no one to highlight the realities of my situation. You're brainwashed into thinking that you still have a chance at United and don't see the bigger picture.

Things came to a head when I was named on the bench for a reserve game against Tranmere Rovers at Gigg Lane which is never a good sign if you've been at a club as a pro for several years. Michael Clegg was picked ahead of me, he was a really good guy who I got on really well with but was a bit of a clone of Gary Neville in the way that he played, so the total opposite of me. He wasn't blessed with great ability but always gave 100% and was built like a bodybuilder. There's a gym in their family and he's Ole's fitness coach at the club now.

I could feel that the likes of Cleggy and John Curtis were moving ahead of me in the pecking order and I didn't feel they were as good as me. When the line-up was read out I was raging, either Jim Ryan or the gaffer would have picked the team and I felt like it took the piss a bit with the number of games I'd played for the reserves. It was a slap in the face. My head was all over the place anyway, I wasn't right mentally and was struggling to cope with all the stress and pressure.

I'd had enough so got up walked out of the dressing room and out of the ground. I sat in my car and phoned my mum to tell her what had happened and she went mental, "John, you get back in there now and go prove them fucking wrong!"

I went back in and made an excuse about going to the toilet or outside for some fresh air when I was asked where I'd been. It was a horrible night and I was brought on when we were losing 1-0. I had the bit between my teeth because my pride had been hurt and felt I had a point to prove. I played in midfield and scored the equaliser soon after coming on. I ran and did a big 'up yours' gesture to the coaches and Jim Ryan as if to say, "Have that you bastard." I realised later that Fergie had been in the crowd that night as well.

Once you're struggling to get a game in the reserves you're being pushed out and my head had completely gone by this point. I didn't care and felt like whatever I did wasn't going to be good enough. I was laid-back anyway but probably took my foot off the pedal even more because I knew my time at United had run its course. I was just being kept around to make up the numbers because they knew I was a half-decent player.

By the end my relationship with Fergie was more distant, I think we both knew that my time was up. I got the impression that he felt he'd done everything he could for me and now it was up to me to forge myself a career in the game. I still respected him and would never go against him. I loved his personality and he would never hold a grudge no matter what you'd done, within reason. He treated players like human beings and that was what set him apart from some of the other managers I played for.

My way out eventually came at the beginning of 1998. I went to the Cliff for a normal day's training and was halfway up the stairs when Jim Ryan came up to me and said the gaffer wanted to speak to me in his office about a move to another club.

Straight away my heart was beating and I was eager to know which club it was. I went up to see him and he offered me another year's contract but said that Everton were interested in signing me but wanted to have a look at me first on a two-week trial to see where my head was at. He said he thought it would be a good move for me and asked if I was up for it.

The fact that it was only a trial irked me but everywhere I went after United I had to go on trial before a club would sign me, probably because I was considered a gamble by most managers due to my reputation. I knew I could turn it on any time I wanted to so I went anyway. I turned up and remember Duncan Ferguson and a few other big hitters being there and we played five-a-side which suited me and I ran the show. Nick Barmby was my kind of player and we ripped it up. I knew I'd done well and straight after Howard Kendall came up to me and said they wanted to sort something out for me to sign for them. My agent was Mel Stein, who was of course Gazza's agent throughout the nineties but that was the only time I actually saw him, when I was in the process of signing for Everton. Fergie hated him, but to be fair he didn't have time for a lot of agents. Mel had a lot of big-name players on his books at the time so had a lot of influence in the game, he was a bit like the Mino Raiola of his day.

I had more regular contact with Shay Trainor, an Irish lad who worked for him and represented John Oster at Everton as well. He was a really nice guy and like a Del Boy sort of character. I remember going with them to Everton's old Bellefield training ground as part of the talks. I wasn't allowed into the actual negotiations which didn't sit right with me so I was left in the back of Mel's car while they went in and sorted it out.

I remember initially asking for about £4000 or £5000 a week but they refused to pay that and negotiated us down. The transfer fee ended up being about £500,000 rising to £1 million depending on appearances and other stuff. I was given £50,000 of that in instalments over the course of a couple of years as a signing-on fee. It was the best offer available so I signed the contract in the back of Mel's car and it was done. I was now an Everton player. There was no real fanfare but I was buzzing to have signed for such a big club with such a great set-up and manager. I was delighted that a manager like Howard Kendall rated me and wanted to sign me.

When I went back to the Cliff for the last time, Fergie

just wished me luck and told me to do my best. I said a quick goodbye to a few of the lads in the reserve team dressing room, got what was left of my stuff and walked out of the place for the last time. There was no gathering round or presentation like some people get when they leave other jobs when they are thanked for their service. You literally just walk out the door, that's the coldness and brutality of football.

I wasn't bothered though, I'd been at United for the best part of nine years but I wasn't emotional about leaving. Deep down I knew that I was leaving behind a cosy little set-up where I wasn't under any real pressure and now I was going to have to pull my finger out. I knew I was going to have to push myself and turn up.

I was looking forward to it though, excited about the opportunity at Everton and the chance to play regular Premier League football.

*All smiles at my 10th birthday party with my Mum in the background getting wound up by my best mate Lenny Sharpe.*

*My family – Mum, Nana, Grandad,
Uncle Jim, Auntie Maureen and Auntie Margaret.*

*We won everything at Pheasant Colts and six of
us from the team made it professionally.*

**MANCHESTER UNITED F.C. 1991-92**

*Back Row (Left to right):* Craig Dean, Gary Neville, Paul Gough, Chris Casper, Andy Noone, Simon Davies, Steven Riley.
*Standing:* Raphael Burke, Eric Harrison, Brian Kidd, Jimmy Curran, Nobby Stiles, Karl Brown.
*Seated:* Mark Rawlinson, Robert Savage, David Beckham, George Switzer, Nicky Butt, John O'Kane, Paul Scholes.

*The Class of 92 in full: Most of the lads in this picture played a part in
winning the FA Youth Cup – something that is often forgotten about.*

*Games against Liverpool were tough no matter what level
they were played at. Here I am playing in an 'A' team
fixture having just gone past Jamie Carragher.
Credit: James A. Thomas*

*It was a great experience to be picked to tour South Africa with the first team
just after they'd won the league in 1993, as was meeting Nelson Mandela.*

*It didn't get much better than playing with these two legends! Celebrating with Keane and Cantona on my first Premier League start away at Middlesbrough - 23rd November 1996.*

*I made it into the first team photo (back row, third from left) just after they'd won the double in 1996, I featured a couple of times that season.*

*In the pool on one of many holidays to Ayia Napa with my pals Neil Taylor, Goughy, Robbo and Chris Holland.*

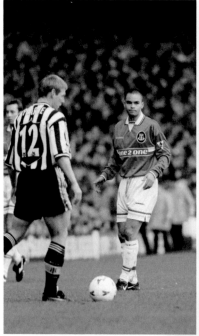

*ABOVE: I loved playing for Everton in the Premier League under Howard Kendall and testing myself against top players. Here I am up against Stuart Pearce and Rob Lee when we played Newcastle.*

*Credit: Everton FC*

*Jumping for Joy: But my time at Bolton and my next club Blackpool wasn't always happy.*

*Me and my mate AB have had some great times together over the years.*

*My three kids: Taelor, Ruby and Vincent who are mine
and Simone's greatest achievements.*

OPPOSITE PAGE
*(Top): Honouring my old coach Eric Harrison at the PFA awards in 2013
where we were also given an award.*
*(Left): With the boss when United played Crystal Palace at Old Trafford in
2017 where I found myself apologising.*
*(Right): With two legends at the Class of 92 reunion – my old mate David
Beckham and my son Taelor.*

*It was good to see the lads at a reunion for Pheasant Colts in 2017 and some of the parents turned up to watch like the old days too.*

*With my best mates JP, Luke Alemanno, Robbo, Andy Bower, Goughy and Declan Ferry on my wedding day in 2013.*

# THRIVING

EVERTON IS A FANTASTIC FOOTBALL club with great fans who are incredibly loyal. They've lived in Liverpool's shadow for so long and had some difficult times but they've got a great history of their own.

I could feel the size of the club at their training ground Bellefield – it had an aura about it. The facilities there were actually better than what I'd been used to at the Cliff which was considered to be state of the art at the time. I didn't come across any nastiness having come from United. The people were brilliant and did everything they could to make me feel welcome, they were really good to me.

Everton were struggling at the bottom of the league and facing relegation when I signed. We knew we were in a sticky situation and we all had to pull together to stay up. The pressure was on because they had been in the top division for as long as anyone could remember so it was a massive step up. In a situation like that I had to believe in myself and the guys around me. We had some good players with experienced heads and a great manager in Howard Kendall who is a legend at that club.

He was brilliant with me and I loved playing for him. You don't really see that much of the manager at any club as the training is often taken by his assistant or the coaches. It's the little interactions you have with them as a player that show that you're in their thoughts and he made me feel special. He'd talk to me, not an awful lot but he'd let me know if he thought that I was doing a good job and it had such a positive impact on me as a player. I felt I had his trust and that pushed me on to do more. It made me feel ten feet tall because to be trusted and shown belief is a massive thing for any player.

Even the best players need an arm round them occasionally and managers have different styles but I wanted that validation sometimes, to feel wanted and liked because it gave me a buzz. It's the same in any job, if you're told you're doing a good job and making a difference it means the world to you.

## Alan Myers – Sky Sports and Former Everton Reporter

*I remember John joining the club, it was a difficult time but I recall Howard Kendall telling me as we were sitting in Bellefield training ground having a cup of tea before doing the press interviews, "He's a top player this lad, he can be world-class for us."*

*I remember thinking that was high praise for such a young player but Howard never spoke like that unless he believed or meant it and John put in a number of important performances at full-back in what was a tense season.*

Walking into the first team dressing room, I faked it in a way. There was some big characters in there like Duncan Ferguson, Slaven Bilic and Dave Watson but on the face of it I was a confident lad who could handle talking to anybody.

Big Dunc was the centre of the dressing room and the club in many ways. He was a funny lad and similar to Roy Keane. Neither of them were psychopaths like people might imagine, they were both funny people who enjoyed the banter with the lads but as soon as they crossed that white line to go out and play they were a completely different animal. It was like a switch had flicked in their head which I never really had as a player.

I got on well with him and he used to like me because I could put in decent crosses for him to get on the end of. We weren't in each other's pockets or anything like that but I think he respected me because I could play.

I remember the club took us to Cyprus for some warm weather training. We went on a night out and ended up in a strip club. Between us we racked up a 20 grand tab and he just paid it at the end of the night. I was still young thinking I was a bit of a lad but underneath I was flapping a bit because I wasn't used to being part of a first team. There was a lot of grit there and we had a great team spirit which was led by Dunc and the other senior pros.

He's still an influential figure at Everton as a coach and did a great job when he was caretaker manager before Carlo Ancelotti took over. He said himself that the club needed the 'best in class' and probably knew that he wasn't in the best position to take the job on a permanent basis.

If he'd have taken it on and they'd struggled then he would have been sacked but he did such a good job in the few games he had it that it will only have boosted his future chances because the fans love him already. You could see that he understood the club and was willing to get into players to get more out of them and make them run harder for the team. He wasn't afraid to make bold decisions and was only interested in the best thing for Everton as a whole and he was the same when I played with him.

He can play on the whole hard man image, like we saw when he stood on the touchline in just his shirt sleeves in the freezing rain at Old Trafford. He probably didn't need to take his coat off but in fairness when I've coached at junior level in all weathers you can be that focussed and absorbed on the game that you don't feel the cold.

Slaven Bilic was great too and people don't realise how good he was. He played in a World Cup semi-final with Croatia the summer after I joined and just read everything whilst looking classy on the ball. I loved playing next to him, and as a young player he always had time for me. He was absolutely brilliant and one of my favourite players there because he used to help me through the games. He was a fans' favourite and we had a good bond on and off the pitch.

There were quite a few younger lads there at the time as well like Don Hutchinson, John Oster, Richard Dunne and Michael Ball so we all sort of stuck together. We were quite a young side anyway and the group of us would often do something together in the afternoon after training like go out for a meal in Liverpool.

I made my debut away at West Ham, I was marking Trevor Sinclair and he scored twice as we drew 2-2 but I don't remember feeling that I'd had a bad game afterwards. I distinctly remember falling on my arse, maybe after doing some sort of slide tackle, and ripping my leg on the pitch and it absolutely killed.

I'd played in a couple of Premier League games at United but this was so much more intense than what I'd been used to playing reserve team football every week. The pace of the game felt like a hundred miles an hour and the atmosphere at Upton Park was typically hostile. I was getting abused left, right and centre by their fans:

"O'Kane, you're shit!"

"United fucking reject!"

West Ham lost something when they moved from that ground. It was a very intimidating place to go because they've got such a great following and I could hear absolutely everything. The fans were right on top of you and they were literally breathing down my neck when I went over to take a throw-in. I could have reached out and touched them.

They had a good side with the likes of Rio Ferdinand and Frank Lampard both having come through their youth system and John Hartson was up-front so it was a very difficult place to go. We'd have been happy to get out with a point, especially with the situation we were in.

I made my home debut a few weeks later in a 0-0 draw against Newcastle at Goodison. Every time I played there the noise in the build-up to the game was massive and the atmosphere was always brilliant. If we gave those fans a little bit of something they'd be right behind us.

It was always very loud and packed to the rafters for every game. In a way I'd come at the worst time when there was a lot of pressure as the club were really struggling but I always felt at home and relaxed playing there because I was playing for a manager who allowed me to enjoy it.

I was being picked in a first team in the Premier League on half-decent money and it just felt like I was riding the crest of a wave. I was playing for a manager who I liked and it was probably the happiest time of my entire football career. I was really enjoying playing football at last after nearly ten years at United where I'd spent most of my time just drifting and going through the motions.

It was a golden era of Premier League football too, every week we were coming up against top teams and big players so I had to be on my game but I enjoyed the challenge and was beginning to more than hold my own.

I remember playing against David Ginola at White Hart Lane. I had a decent game and I don't remember him taking me on. He was a clever player who used to drop deep onto the halfway line, we drew that game 1-1 so it was another decent point and I just wish I'd got his shirt.

I picked up a suspension quite early on for number of bookings, some of which had been carried over from when I was at Bradford earlier in the season. I did like a tackle but there was this perception of me that I wasn't a big tackler. I could mark players out of the game but a lot of the time I felt like I could just dink it over somebody and didn't need to dive in. It's about timing and positioning, you rarely see some of the best defender's tackle because they don't need to, except maybe last ditch.

The mentality in this country is still very up and at 'em and fans and coaches want players to get stuck in. Mindlessly diving into tackles wasn't really my game and maybe if I'd have played abroad it would have been seen differently.

If I'd have been playing nowadays I think I would have been looked upon more favourably with the impact the likes of Pep Guardiola has had on the game in this country. More technical players are celebrated in the modern game whereas when I played it was more about getting stuck in which I could do as well if I needed – I picked up a few yellow cards that season.

My suspension meant I missed the Merseyside derby at Anfield but I was in the stands to see us draw 1-1 with Big Dunc scoring our goal. It would have been brilliant to play in that game, the noise from the crowd was so loud and it was a pleasure to be there and see it at close quarters. Liverpool weren't great at the time but Everton were always seen as being that little bit inferior.

We weren't one of the great Everton sides by any means but we were a decent team and just didn't have any big stars. Nick Barmby and Michael Madar were the only ones who were particularly creative and had a bit of flair about them. We were just hard-working and we played for the manager.

My first win for the club came in a 1-0 triumph over Blackburn Rovers at Goodison before we played Leeds at home a few weeks later going into the final run of games and really needing a result. I had probably my best game for the club in a 2-0 win where I won man of the match.

Leeds were a good side with some great individual players. I was excited beforehand because I knew I'd be marking Harry Kewell, who was the young darling of the Premier League at that time. It was a tough job because he was fast and tricky as well. He was another player who got labelled from early in his career for being a bit soft and I knew I had to rattle him and try and get him to come at me.

It's funny the conversations you can have with opposition players, especially as a full-back marking a winger because you're usually stood next to him for most of the game. It's just small talk like you get in any office or factory floor. One of us might say, "where are you going tonight mate?" If it's a healthy rivalry and you respect each other you tend to help each other up after tackles. Other times it gets more heated and can turn nasty or I might try and lure him into a false sense of security by being really nice and then smash him. It all depends on the nature of the game.

That day I decided to come out and challenge him and I remember saying in his ear, "Come on, take me on. Run at me, let's see what ya got." He couldn't do it and I'm not sure he got past me all day. I remember coming off at the end of the game feeling like I'd really accomplished something.

Lucas Radebe got sent off after 17 minutes and I set up our second goal with a cross from the right-hand side for Big Dunc to head home. I was a decent crosser of the ball, I used to practice with Beckham when we were young players at United and I had good technique. I always knew playing for Everton that if I got forward to look for Dunc in the box and he'd always be there. It was a great moment and that game was one of the best I played.

It was a massive result for us going into the final run of games where it was still touch and go. Three points is huge in a relegation battle and I can't describe the feeling of coming off the pitch at the end of the game knowing we've won and I'd played well. Any footballer will tell you, it's unbelievable knowing the fans are buzzing and there's no better feeling.

Many will have experienced that winning feeling playing at grassroots level or Sunday league, but when you're playing in the Premier League it's frightening and I'd never really had it before at that level; playing every week in games that really mattered to the fans who followed us everywhere in their thousands and feeling really comfortable in my own skin. My tics were under control and everything just felt right. Everton were the only club I played for who picked up on my twitching and offered support. I remember one of the physios, a bloke called Jimmy Comer, saying to me, "John, are you alright mate? You're twitching, do you need some help or to go see someone?"

"Nah Jim, I'm okay. Don't worry about it."

I just shrugged it off. Mental health awareness then isn't what it is now and in a way he was ahead of his time for even asking.

With just two games left we went to play Arsenal at

Highbury. They battered us 4-0 and they were a great side with Adams, Viera and Anelka all featuring and this was the year they beat United to the league title. They were actually crowned champions after that game which was also Ian Wright's last match for them at Highbury. They were too good for us and Marc Overmars was an absolute nightmare to mark. I was quick but I just could not stay with him. I still have nightmares about him spinning me for pace and that low centre of gravity that he had - I'd never seen anything like it. He'd do a couple of strides and would already be ten yards ahead of me. It was ridiculous and there were plenty of other full backs who got rinsed by him. As usual I enjoyed the challenge but got nowhere near him. He was world-class.

As a defender you'd rather play against someone with good technical ability like Ginola than the pure pace Overmars had because even if you got tight he could still spin you and if you gave him space he'd just knock it past you and be away. The best thing to do with a player like that is clatter him before he gets going but again that's easier said than done. I don't think I even touched him that day and he scored twice.

I remember running back over the halfway line and elbowing Emmanuel Petit in the head. They replayed the game on *Match of the Day* a while ago and you can just see him lying on the floor. He went mental and I think he went off not long after that. I think I got booked because the linesman saw it but nowadays it would have been a straight red, especially with VAR.

I got brought off at half-time with a couple of the other lads when the gaffer changed the system because we were losing and watching from the bench in the second half, you obviously don't want to be losing but in a way it was almost enjoyable as a spectacle to watch Arsenal play and see them win the league in that way purely as a football fan. Highbury was bouncing that day, as an opposition player it was a claustrophobic and intimidating place to go. The pitch felt tiny and it was like I couldn't breathe. It was a grand old stadium and you could tell that they were a very classy club.

We couldn't admire how good Arsenal were for too long though because heading into the final game of the season we were a point behind Bolton so it wasn't in our hands. They would play Chelsea while we'd be at home to Coventry City. I remember there being concern that Chelsea wouldn't field their strongest side because they had a European final to prepare for but as a player I could only concentrate on my game and hope for the best.

At the time, we knew we were struggling and in a battle but the whole gravity of the situation that the club could get relegated and the potential consequences of it didn't really dawn on me. I was playing for the badge and to get results, trying my best. In my mind we were always going to stay up, I didn't think about if we might go down because it was my job to make sure that didn't happen.

I felt the pressure a little bit more in the build-up to a game like that though. When we were going to training or out and about in Liverpool we'd bump into fans who were quick to remind us how big a deal it was.

"Come on John, you better win for us on Saturday."

The fans had really taken to me since I'd joined the club. I think they knew I was a decent player but also that I needed shaking every now and then because I was a bit laid-back. To them Everton is everything. It's what their life is built around and I just wanted to do it for them. That game was more about them than us; we were just representing their club. It was probably the biggest game of my career.

I was obviously nervous beforehand but I felt at the height of my powers because I'd had a good run of games playing at the highest level. I felt good mentally and physically and I trusted us as a team that we'd do what was needed on the day. The atmosphere was ridiculous and if you watch it back when they replay it on Sky you can see the fans holding their radios listening to what was happening in Bolton's game.

Gareth Farrelly put us ahead early on with a great goal from outside the box and we were pretty comfortable before Nick Barmby missed a penalty in the second half which would have killed the game off. With about five minutes left I took a few extra touches close to my own box after the keeper had passed it out to me. I should have got it and put it down the side but I did a little jink past the centre-forward and casually played it back to the goalie. I heard later that Kendall had gone berserk on the bench, "What's he fucking doing!"

Looking back now, in that situation I should have played safe and belted it. Being honest, if I were the manager I would probably have dropped someone like me for that game because you just want your team to go out there, don't fuck anything up and take as few risks as possible. In a way my game was all about risk, I didn't always want to play the easy ball and would try things as that was just in my nature. I guess it comes down to making the right decisions which is something I wasn't always deemed as doing. I wanted to be more of a risk taker and express myself. I respect some managers looking at me as a bit of a risk so I was a bit surprised that I played that day.

Late in the game I also touched a low shot onto the

post that if it had of got a bigger deflection could have ended up in the back of the net. Those are the margins you play with and it's scary when you think about it. I'm glad I'm not remembered for scoring the own goal that sent Everton down!

Dion Dublin scored a late equaliser for them but by then we knew that a draw would be enough as the message from the bench and the crowd was that Chelsea were pretty comfortable against Bolton and we'd stay up on goal difference. It was just a case of waiting for the final whistle in what was an unbelievably tense few minutes and when you're on the pitch it feels like it's never going to come.

When it did the whole ground just erupted. It was crazy, the feeling of sheer relief. Fucking hell! The fans were on the pitch and I wanted to stay out there and celebrate with them forever. It was a great thing to be a part of, absolute quality. We got mobbed and at first I couldn't really comprehend what was going on. I remember jumping on one of the other lads and not knowing what to do with myself, after all the build-up, the exhilaration I felt was just incredible.

It's a weird thing to celebrate just staying up and being the fourth worst team in the league but for the club and those fans it meant absolutely everything. If we'd have gone down I don't know what would have happened because many clubs that have been relegated from the Premier League have slid right down or even out of the Football League.

I swapped shirts with Dion Dublin at the end of the game which was a nice little memento and I've still got it. I must have gone out that night to celebrate but I've no recollection of it, it was probably the highlight of my career.

We'd done it, we'd stayed up by the skin of our teeth and there was another season in the Premier League to look forward to. I was enjoying my football playing for a good manager who liked me alongside a decent set of team-mates. I was playing well, beginning to prove that I could cut it in the Premier League and most importantly I was happy. Which is all I wanted in life.

I remember a story in one of the papers saying that if I carried on playing as I was I could be rivalling Gary Neville for his right-back spot in the England squad. In half a season I had gone from someone whose career seemed to be drifting in United reserves, to helping to save one of the biggest clubs in English football from relegation and now I was being talked about as a potential international! I didn't take too much notice of this back then but I often think about it now.

I remember at the end of the season as I was getting ready to go off for the summer they were talking about sorting a new contract for me which would have been the one that really set me up on decent money as an established member of the squad but when I look back on it now and with the way things turned out, there's a part of me that wishes my career had ended that day celebrating with those fans on the pitch at Goodison Park.

## LAZY BASTARD

I WAS LYING ON A BEACH IN AYIA NAPA enjoying my summer holiday when I received the news that would send my football career into a downward spiral. I picked up a copy of *The Sun* and the headline on the sports section just jumped from the page.

'KENDALL SACKED AS EVERTON MANAGER'

I was gutted.

"You're fucked now aren't you," my mates laughed.

I hoped not. The club were in the process of offering me a new deal and had appointed Walter Smith who'd won loads of league titles with Rangers in Scotland. Archie Knox would be coming as his assistant and he knew me as a young player at United when he'd been Fergie's assistant so understood my game and what I was about. I knew I'd have to more or less start again and prove myself but I hoped that I'd be given a fair shot by the new manager.

All that went out the window on our first meeting. I'd come out of the boot room at Bellefield and was walking up the stairs to go out and train and he passed me on the way down. The new manager collared me and just said, "I've heard you're a lazy bastard."

"It's nice to meet you as well," was my response. Which looking back probably wasn't the right way of dealing with it but what could I say to that? Like I say, some players are given a label early on in their career and it's difficult to shake off. Mud sticks.

He might have been saying it in jest or trying to test me to see how I'd react but my back went up straight away and from his point of view it probably worked for him.

That pre-season I trained as hard as anybody else because I wanted to be in the team, but when the campaign got underway I wasn't playing and it became obvious that he wanted to bring in his own people and players who were loyal to him. It's understandable for any new manager looking to make their mark at a club to try and put their own stamp on the team. My issue was the way that he went about it and the way I was treated.

There was Alec Cleland from Rangers in my position who was a lovely guy to be fair but I didn't feel that he was any better than I was. He was a typical hard-working player, a seven out of ten every week which was fair enough, but I knew I was a better technical player.

David Weir also came from Rangers in defence and David Unsworth was brought back to the club. He brought in Marco Materazzi at centre-half who I wasn't keen on. Zinedine Zidane famously head-butted him in the World Cup final and to be honest I wasn't surprised. He was a bit snidey and most of the other players didn't particularly like him either.

There was also Olivier Dacourt in midfield who went on to play for Leeds who was an absolute gentleman and a very good technical player to be fair, probably too technical to be playing in that side.

If you're on the wrong end of a situation like that in football it's often an unpleasant place to be and you can become bitter and even resent your team-mates in a way. I felt angry all the time and going into training wasn't fun because it was like my whole existence or job was pointless because there was no game to look forward to at the end of the week.

Walter was the sort of manager who would completely blank any players who weren't in his plans rather than treat them like human beings which is all 99% of us want. Some can treat you like babies which is what I always hated and if you dared to answer back or question the way things were done he couldn't handle the challenge to his authority.

It soon became obvious that not only did he not fancy me as a player but it was also becoming personal between us. I remember one time in training where we were doing boxes with one or two players in the middle and we were taking the piss out of them a bit and nutmegging them, nothing disrespectful just having a bit of a laugh and a joke:

All of a sudden I hear, "O'Kane what the fuck are you laughing at? Get inside!"

I'm not sure why I was singled out because I wasn't doing anything any of the other lads weren't. I can only think that he thought it looked bad on the lads in the middle who were in his team. I stood up to him, refused to go anywhere and then trained for the rest of the session but the damage had already been done.

I was made to train with the kids because he didn't want me anywhere near him. They had a good youth team around that time and won the FA Youth Cup. There were some good lads there like Jamie Milligan and Danny Cadamarteri and we had a good laugh but as a senior pro it's not where you want to be and it's very demoralising.

All the enjoyment and momentum I'd got from the previous season had been lost and my relationship with football at that point was probably the worst it had ever been. That's considering that I was never someone who lived and breathed the game in the first place, it hurt though.

One day I decided to confront the situation head-on. I knocked on his office door like I'd done dozens of times before with Fergie and Howard Kendall for a chat. I walked in and he half looked up at me over his desk while he was doing something:

"What do you actually have against me? I done well last season and I want to play for you and this club."

He just stared at me and couldn't give me a proper answer. He was caught completely off-guard.

"Get the fuck out of my office."

I remember walking out and almost bursting into tears because I knew then that my Everton career was over and there was no way back. It hurt me and probably unsettled him because you won't get a lot of players openly questioning a manager to try and sort something. The best managers can deal with all different types of players but he didn't have that in his locker.

I hated him and still do because to me he wrecked my Everton career and treated me like shit just because he wanted to bring his own people in. I've never seen him since and don't know what I'd do if I bumped into him. He was a bully who was old fashioned and set in his ways. When I speak to Everton fans now they always have positive things to say about my time there but often some will comment that I had a few good games for them and then just disappeared which is down to him.

## Alan Myers

*When Walter Smith came in it was clear he didn't fancy John as a player. I think he had the players in mind he wanted in his defence and that didn't include John and a few others! It was a difficult time for the likes of John and Gareth Farrelly at that point.*

*Something which always sticks with me about John was his*

*laid-back attitude, a player who never seemed to get too overexcited or too down about anything. I remember being in the dressing room for a reserve game when John was out of the first team picture. Andy Holden was the reserve coach, they'd been beaten and Andy gave them a tongue lashing and I remember him saying to me how frustrated he was with John in particular because he knew he was a very good player,* **"If I went in and told him that football was cancelled forever, he would just get his coat and go home,"** *Holden told me. To say John took it all in his stride would be an understatement, a good guy though!*

There was another incident where me and John Oster were sat in the stands watching a game. He'd been discarded as well so neither of us were in the best of moods. We were just having a laugh and talking watching the game when David Unsworth I think it was shanked the ball out of play.

We had a little giggle as you do but nothing disrespectful. I never sat on the bench or in the stands and hoped that whoever was playing ahead of me had a bad game because I didn't care about football enough to do that. Obviously you don't want them to have a blinder and score a hat-trick but you'd be pleased for them on a human level if they did.

Someone in the directors' box reported us for not paying attention to the game. It got back to the manager who got us down in the dressing room afterwards and blitzed the pair of us.

"YOU'RE NEVER PLAYING FOR THIS CLUB AGAIN!"

By this point I'd stopped caring and just stood there and took it. It was almost funny. I ended up going out on loan to Burnley to try and play a few games because it was another chance to work with Stan Ternent again. He'd just taken the job there and knew my character and that

I had good ability. Football is all about opinions and who a manager wants in their team, that's literally all it comes down to.

I went there and did alright but nothing special, it wasn't like when I played for him at Bury and there was the motivation to win the league. In the couple of months or so that I was there I played eight games in the old Division 2 and we lost six of them so they were struggling a bit at the time.

It was a very old school club as well. I live not far from Burnley now and have had jobs there. It's a proper working-class town with good parts and bad parts but at the time I didn't have any particular connection with the club itself. I was just there to help Stan out and play a few games so the fans didn't really take to me and you could hear the comments from the stands:

"Get back to United you fucking reject!"

They have a bit of a rivalry with United so I was up against it already and when you're supposed to be one of the better players the fans tend to take it out on you when things aren't going well. I had no real motivation to play for their club other than to get out of Everton training with the kids for a bit and I think they picked up on that. I was just there to fill a spot which was what Stan needed and it was a bit of a comedown from playing in the Premier League a few months before.

## Stan Ternent – Burnley manager 1998-2004

*John had done unbelievably well for me at Bury to the extent that when I took the job at Burnley and he'd fallen out of favour at Everton he came and played for me there as well. Everybody said that his time at Turf Moor was less successful but I didn't think it was. He was the same John to me and did the job I asked of him.*

They're a different club now to what they were when I was there and have done very well to get into the Premier League and stay there. It's a well-run club where the fans are loyal to their team and it's built on good values. You have to respect that but for me at the time I just wasn't in the best frame of mind.

Back at Everton Walter Smith might not have liked me or trusted me and the feeling was mutual, but he knew I could handle playing in big games. When his team started to pick up a few injuries in early 1999 I started to get a bit of a look-in with the first team because he needed a spot filling in defence. Mentally that was difficult after being frozen out for so long because I had to switch my feelings off that I fucking hated him and try and play for him. Not easy.

I came off the bench in FA Cup wins over Ipswich and Coventry before being given my first start for the club in nearly a year in the next round against Newcastle at St James's Park. It's a massive ground and I've been back there since to watch United and it was only then, from the vantage point of the away fans section up in the Gods, that I appreciated how big a place it is.

We got beat 4-1 but the thing I remember most about that game is stopping Alan Shearer scoring. The cross came in and I was running towards the back post with him behind me, everyone who saw him play knows what would usually happen next, he'd lift off, tower over the top of you and the ball would be in the back of the net.

I could feel him coming behind me, thundering like a horse but I held him and flicked it over his head for a corner. I ended up in the net instead of the ball but I recall a brief moment of pride thinking, 'I've just stopped Alan Shearer from scoring a goal.'

It was a great moment because he would be my first-choice number nine of the Premier League era. He was lethal and as an out and out pure goalscorer he was the best. He wasn't the tallest but he could really leap and was a powerful header of the ball.

Then I played in a 2-1 win over Blackburn Rovers at Ewood Park before being picked on the right wing to play against United at Old Trafford. That was strange in itself, they knew I could play in midfield if needed but I think it was more a defensive approach to try and help contain them because they were flying in what was the treble winning season. They were probably expecting to have to deal with Giggsy down that side but he didn't play in the end.

I'd been gone nearly 18 months and I was a bit nervous about going back. I remember walking in and seeing Kath on the front desk and all the same faces are there wishing me well. I bumped into Fergie after we'd got off the coach and we shook hands: "Good to see you John. Good luck today."

Warming up I got a little clap from the United fans when my name was read out which settled me down a little bit but once the game started they were just on a different level to us. When you leave a club like United your fitness levels drop slightly because you're not training and playing at the same intensity as the top teams do.

At times it was like being in a dream. I did alright and remember putting a few crosses into the box but I just remember them being so sharp. It hurt in a way because part of me knew that if things had worked out differently I could have been playing for them rather than against them.

I just tried to take in the surroundings and enjoy the game being back at Old Trafford. It was like saying goodbye to the place and Everton as well because I knew that was coming to an end. I was never really a first team player at United but it was nice to get a bit of acknowledgement from the fans who'd watched me play hundreds of games for them at all levels since the age of 14.

I remember hearing odd words of encouragement from the United fans down the side I was playing which was really nice of them. I got brought off after an hour and I got a decent reception from both sets of fans which I really appreciated walking off. We ended up getting beat 3-1 with Ole Gunnar Solskjaer, Gary Neville and Becks all scoring for them. It was fitting really as that turned out to be my last game for Everton. Once Walter Smith's preferred players were back from injury, I was back training with the kids again.

With no football of my own to concentrate on apart from the odd reserve game I had plenty of time to watch the United games when they were going for the treble as a fan and even though I'd left I still wanted them to win the league. Most of my mates in Bury where I lived were United fans and I watched the Champions League final against Bayern Munich in a pub with a few of the lads. When Solskjaer scored the winner the place went mental and we fell over a table celebrating. There were drinks flying everywhere and it was just madness.

I loved it. I'd played and trained with most of the lads in that team and there was no bitterness. I was happy for them and what they'd achieved. They were great players and there was a small part of me that wondered if it could have been me but there's obviously a reason why I was no longer there. Fergie had offered me another contract when I'd signed for Everton so if I'd have stayed I might even have played in a few games that season but my time had been up and now 18 months later at Everton with Walter Smith treating me like I didn't exist that was looking dead in the water too. I was in a bad place with how things were going football-wise and beginning to wonder if I had any sort of long-term future in the game.

# LIVING IN A BUBBLE

EVERY YEAR, ONCE THE SEASON HAD finished, there was one thing on most of the lad's minds – where are we going on holiday?

It's a long season so the chance to get away for a few weeks from the usual routine and enjoy a bit of freedom always appealed. It's not like you can just book time off over the course of the year like most jobs, so you always tried to make the most of it.

I think I spent nearly every summer when I was playing abroad. You'd sometimes be away from when the season finished and just come back for pre-season or you'd go somewhere for two weeks then come back and go somewhere else.

Ayia Napa was the place that most players used to go in the nineties and I remember going for the first time with Goughy, Robbo and Matt Carbon who I'd played with at Pheasant Colts and played at Derby County and West Brom. We were all a bit naïve in our late teens and I think Matt went home after a few days as it was so far out of his comfort zone. I fell in love with this Norwegian girl big time in the two weeks we were over there and that was my life sorted; I wanted to move to Norway or move her over here but it didn't work out for obvious reasons - crazy.

I was out in Napa about four years running. I remember meeting up with Michael Gray one year who had been at United but got released and ended up at Sunderland. That was an experience because he was mental and I remember meeting him in the square at the start of a night out and he turned up in these pants which were half leather half jeans and no top on. He had his long blonde hair and looked ridiculous. He's another player who was maybe a bit misunderstood, a really nice guy just a bit flashy and we had some crazy times together.

Another time I remember me, Goughy and Robbo playing volleyball on the beach with Jamie Redknapp and his brother. He'd just got into Liverpool's first team and all the girls just flocked to him because he was a very good-looking lad, like an Adonis. It was a footballer's paradise and there would be loads of them out there but we usually just did our own thing. They were good times.

## Steve Robinson

*We went to Ayia Napa umpteen times and have some great memories just being young lads.*

*John was always the cool one when we went away whereas I'd always burn because I'm pasty white and I'd look at him and he'd be bronzed up. He'd chuck a t-shirt on, make hardly any effort and he looked a million dollars. Put it this way he never struggled in attracting attention from the opposite sex.*

*He was a bit of a wallflower in many respects and liked to be on the edge of things. We'd all be getting pissed up, dancing and messing around but it didn't really come naturally to John. I don't think John was really a drinker looking back but he mucked in and you kind of just go along with it at that age.*

*One time we all copied David Beckham and went out in sarongs and a vest just to take the Mick really. Everyone got wind of it and it ended up being friends of friends turning out until we had about 40 of us sat in a restaurant somewhere all wearing the same daft outfit. There must be a photo somewhere.*

*We had some cracking golf holidays in Southern Spain and*

*the Costa del Sol. Seeing Stan Boardman doing stand-up in a bar in Fuengirola was another highlight, he was brilliant and had just got out the shower.*

I remember doing a few press-ups on the hotel balcony to try and keep my fitness or going for a run on the beach but it never used to last because it'd either be too hot or I'd be hungover. Most nights we didn't get in till five or six in the morning, then you're asleep on the beach for most of the day before going out again that night.

I put a bit of weight on which would be run off when I went back for pre-season but nothing excessive. I was naturally fit anyway so I knew I'd work it off in the endless running we'd have to do where we wouldn't see a ball in the first couple of weeks.

When most people think of being a professional footballer they have this vision of it being the perfect lifestyle. A lot of people don't really understand that a footballer's life away from the pitch during the season can be very boring. It's more or less the same regimented routine where you train all week, play on a Saturday and then you might have a night out with the lads after the game before it all starts again the following week.

Once I'd moved out of my mum and step-dad's and got my own place in Radcliffe I led quite a lonely life, so once I got home from training I needed to find ways to fill the rest of the day. I'd sometimes have a round of golf in the afternoon which I only really started to get into when I was a bit older. Other than that, there wasn't much else to do apart from sitting around watching TV or videos and sometimes I'd have a bet on the horses.

I had a couple of steady girlfriends whilst I was playing, the first I was with on and off for about ten years. Her name was Sarah Paget and I'd met her at Cheadle Hulme High School, looking back now it was more of a social thing for us both and I remember going to weddings and other functions with her. She was a nice girl and wasn't a gold-digger or anything like that.

She lived over in Bramhall in quite a posh area and her mum and dad were both brilliant people who took to me. We went away to quite a few places together and it worked because we weren't in each other's pockets all the time and only saw each other once or twice a week. We were more friends in hindsight and it just kind of ran its course.

Later on in my career I lived with a girl called Tess Page who I'd met on a night out in Blackpool. She was a student at Oxford University and we got on really well. She was studying Biochemistry so we didn't have a great deal in common and she was away at university a lot of the time so I didn't see her that often.

I had a lot of time for her family and we ended up getting a place together near Poulton-le-Fylde which was a converted barn - a beautiful house. I loved it up there and we had a good life but we drifted apart in the end, there were no bad feelings and I'm still in touch with her occasionally now.

Where I lived in Radcliffe was a few doors down from a lad called Lee Bower. He'd sometimes come round in the evening and we'd have some food and watch DVD's. I didn't really socialise with any team-mates from United as they weren't in my circle and a lot of the lads at Everton lived closer to Liverpool.

One night me and Lee went to a club where he introduced me to his brother Andy who was really into golf and we've been best mates ever since.

## Andy Bower

*I first met John when he was still at United. He lived a couple of doors down from my brother and I just got a phone call from Lee one day asking if I'd take John out for a round of golf because after he finished training they just used to get a KFC and watch films all day.*

*I was managing a nightclub at the time and they came in together. I walked over and Lee introduced us, John was sat down facing me and just stuck his arm out. I remember thinking, 'Who is this pretentious arsehole?' but we hit it off. I took to him and he took to me, when you get to know John you realise he's very shy and at first it may come across as arrogance. He's come out of his shell now though and I think he's found his vocation on Twitter.*

*I always got the impression that he never really enjoyed the 'job', if that's what you can call it, of being a professional footballer. He always had an issue with people telling him what to do and I think he found the whole lifestyle very regimented, you were told what time to get up, what time to go to bed, you were told what time to train and I don't think he ever really got to grips with it.*

*I went everywhere with him and used to take him to training just for a bit of moral support. I remember when he signed for Everton he called me asking what kind of car I wanted because he thought they were going to give him £6000 a week. Then he rang me back half an hour later, I think they'd gone for a break and Fergie had got involved telling Everton to give him £1500 a week max! I know John felt he'd been done over!*

*He did really well that first season at Everton and I think he was the fans' player of the year. There was a good atmosphere around the club and they really took to him but he ended up leaving because he fell out with Walter Smith and that was the pattern throughout his career.*

*When I used to go watch him I'd get there about 1pm and sit in the players' lounge. The pints were really cheap at Everton at 50p so I used to be absolutely shedded by the time he came out. I remember one game later on when he was at Bolton where he did his ankle in. I've had about ten pints waiting for him and neither of us could drive because his foot was in this massive boot. We've had some great times over the years.*

At the time I just wanted to enjoy life and was earning decent money but nothing like what players get today. Nowadays players are on ten or twenty grand a week before they've even played in the first team or average players are on a hundred grand a week. When I played you had to be a regular in the first team at a top club to be on the big money and the boom was only really just beginning.

I wasn't a massive gambler, not by footballer's standards anyway, and never had a problem with it. I could have stopped any time that I wanted – it was just something to do to beat the boredom and a bit of excitement to get through those long afternoons. I remember putting £1000 or £500 each way on a horse which is crazy now when I think about it but back then my attitude was that if it came in then great, if not then I was earning decent money so it wouldn't impact me too much anyway.

I'd first gone into a bookies with Keith Gillespie when we were both apprentices at United. I didn't have a clue what I was doing and remember looking at the boards to try and make sense of them while he was betting on everything. I think he won quite a lot of money that day but he had that streak in him where he wasn't happy winning.

Quite a few players from my generation ended up with quite serious problems with gambling like Keith and I can understand why. Online betting wasn't really a thing then so it was all done over the phone which is dangerous in itself because it didn't feel like real money until they came round with the bill.

I wouldn't say I was completely stupid with money but I definitely could have been better with it. I had enough to keep me going and I was comfortable but I was always chasing it, trying to get more which I didn't really need. I wanted it just to have an easy life and in some ways I wish I'd have handled it better.

Steve Robinson had a decent career in the Football League and never got that massive contract but he handled his money better than I did. He never really splashed out on fancy cars or anything extravagant whilst I was buying BMWs and he questioned why I was doing it once and I bit his head off.

"Robbo, what the fuck has it got to do with you how I spend my money? Let me spend it how I want to."

He still reminds me of that now. He's got a good little family and is comfortable. I really wish I'd have listened to him, at the time I just wanted to live my life and enjoy it whilst he was staying in and not going out. I never gave a thought for the future and I came from a background where we never had any money to save so I just used to get it and spend it. There's a balance to be had at the end of the day but at the time I just lived for each day.

I liked my cars; I had a top of the range silver BMW Convertible with two doors which was my favourite and cost me £36,000 which in those days was a lot of money. It had a grey leather interior and it was a beautiful car. You sometimes see them around now and they're worth about £2000 at best but at the time I absolutely loved it. Only problem was it ended up getting stolen.

Someone had tried to nick it before but it had an

immobiliser fitted so they couldn't move it. So they tried to key it and go in through the door. I woke up one morning to go to training and there was a big hole in the door. My mum used to work in pubs so she knew a lot of bouncers and word gets round in those sort of circles. She found who it was and it was a young kid, I don't know this for a fact but I heard that they caught him and hit his hand with a hammer. That's how brutal my mum was and even though I wasn't a kid anymore she'd have done anything to protect me.

When it eventually got stolen I was on holiday in Marbella playing golf. I was with Sarah at the time and had left the car with her to look after and got her insured on it. I got a call as I was ready to tee off and it was Sarah to say it had been nicked whilst parked outside her house. All of the lads were pissing themselves laughing, she'd tried to sort it all out for me with the insurance company but they wouldn't pay out because it wasn't parked on the driveway at my house in Radcliffe where it was registered which seemed ridiculous.

I wasn't too pissed off because my attitude was that it was just a car so I enjoyed the rest of my holiday. When I got back I was then told that as I wasn't insured I had to pay the car off in full as I'd got it on a lease deal. I got another one more or less straight away but I had to pay off the rest of the £36,000 in one instalment. Even when you're earning good money like I was at Everton that's still quite a hit to take and that was where most of my £50,000 signing-on bonus went, on that car!

One of the positives of the kind of money I was earning was that it allowed me to financially support my mum after she'd done the same for me for so many years. She was still working menial jobs so I helped her out where I could.

She gave me everything so it was the natural thing to do, money meant nothing to me and she'd pay her own way as much as she could.

I paid the deposit on a house for her, she paid the mortgage but I gave her the leg up because in my eyes she came first and that was the bond we had being an only child and single mum. She could have easily got rid of me or put me up for adoption when I was a baby, especially being a mixed-race kid from a white family, and the way that attitudes were different then but she fought to keep me and bring me up.

I found the whole football lifestyle more and more monotonous the further I went through my career because you can't do stuff that normal people can. You can't just go out for a couple of drinks on a Friday night because you have to be in bed for a game the next day. You have to watch what you eat and can't enjoy things like other people can because you're always thinking about your fitness and the next game. It takes a lot of commitment and dedication to even have half a career.

You live quite a sheltered life really. You're told where to go, what to say, what to eat and what to wear. You become institutionalised and it's like being part of a cult where you need to conform or you're just cast aside.

There is a disconnect with the outside world too which has only grown since I played and now the divide between fans and players is frightening. It's easier for players to come across as big time with their social media accounts and clothing ranges when they're not that good on the pitch and I think that doesn't go down well with the fans.

Players are put on a pedestal like superstars but they're

just normal people. I was never a big star but I never turned someone down who asked for an autograph just out of common courtesy. It's nice to be appreciated but it doesn't make you any better than the people that you're signing an autograph for. I remember when I was at United Cantona used to be stood there signing for ages every day. Even players like myself who weren't really anybody would have to do it. Driving out of the Cliff after training I used to keep my head down because I didn't think any of the fans waiting would be bothered about getting mine and I'd be embarrassed if they did ask but they'd bang on the window of your car to get you to stop and sometimes I could be there for an hour.

I've never minded having a chat with fans on the odd occasion they recognise me. I don't go out of my way to talk about football to anybody but if they bring it up I don't mind having a conversation. Sometimes when people have come up to me saying I used to be at United I have denied it, I want people to talk to me for me, not what I used to do for a living.

Mental health is another issue in football and has only really become a thing in the last few years, but it's always been there and there were players who struggled with it. One lad I know suffered a mental breakdown due to the pressures he was under when he was playing and from those around him. It's a brutal business and you've got to be tough to survive.

If the coaches or other players saw a chink in their armour, they'd just go for certain lads. There were ridiculously talented players who struggled to cope in that brutal environment and there wasn't any help for them at all. You had to be strong mentally and the coaches' attitude was that any negative or unpleasant experiences built character and you could expect far worse if you made it into the first team.

I obviously had my own stuff to deal with and I think team-mates and managers always knew there was something 'different' about me. I always knew I was autistic and I just tried to get on with it but it was a mental drain because there's a lot of other stuff that naturally comes with trying to play football at a high level. There's a lot of uncertainty and anxiety; you worry about your form, the team's performance if things aren't going well or you're in a tight situation, you could get injured or be worried about a new manager coming in and if they're going to like you or why they're not picking you in the team.

Then there's the pressure of playing; the nerves, the highs and lows, fighting to get results for the fans and every mistake being scrutinised. You can play in front of hostile crowds and there are times when your own fans turn on you. It's not easy and you've got to be tough mentally because a lot of the time it's step up or step out.

I got a reputation throughout my career that I couldn't deal with the pressure but I don't believe that. It was more that I struggled to suppress my own demons and that's what a lot of people didn't understand. I could usually deal with the pressure of playing and I had some good games playing against top class players over the course of my career but it's not the same for everyone.

Mental health is a massive thing now and it's good that it's being talked about in the game but there's been a lot of people who've been damaged from their experiences playing in previous years because it was just the norm. Nowadays the PFA offer help to current and former players but 20 years ago there was nothing at all. If you were seen as weak you weren't going to last and the game chews you up and spits you out.

I say it a lot but life as a professional footballer is really just like living in a big bubble and as I got into my mid-twenties I knew I would have to burst it sooner or later.

## NEARLY MAN

I HAD TO GET OUT OF EVERTON AND AWAY from Walter Smith so when Bolton enquired about taking me on trial I had nothing to lose. I turned up and played in a practice game for the reserves against the first team. I knew I had to turn it on so I chose to be in midfield that day and ran the show. I remember us getting a free-kick about 30 yards out and just thinking, "I'm having this!" I put it in the top corner past Jussi Jaaskelainen and Sam Allardyce had seen enough. He asked me to sign straight away.

Bolton was supposed to be a fresh start for me. It was a North West club so there were no issues with travel or having to move and at the time they were on the up. They'd moved to the new stadium at the Reebok a couple of years before and had a decent squad with the clear aim of achieving promotion to the Premier League.

Big Sam was a decent manager who was old school like Howard Kendall and he seemed to have no issues with man managing me at first or understanding my character. He was very bright, not like what people might think and if he had a more exotic name he'd probably be seen differently in the game because in a lot of ways he was ahead of his time.

He was big into stats and Prozone was relatively new at the time but he and the club really bought into it. I always remember him saying to me after I'd set up a goal and put five or six crosses into the box for Dean Holdsworth that

I should have been making another five crosses a game because that's what the data was telling him. I remember being amazed with how on the ball he was with stuff like that and we used to have a lot of meetings to discuss it. It was all high-tech stuff and they were one of the first clubs to use it.

I got on well with Phil Brown as well who was Sam's assistant. He'd been a right-back himself and knew I could play. We had some good laughs in the first year or so that I was there. We had quite a good technical side and they were building a good team. There were a few Scandinavian lads there like Michael Johansen, Bo Hansen, Claus Jensen and Per Frandsen.

A young Eidur Gudjohnsen played up-front, he was quality and a bit of a fans' favourite. He reminded me of Anthony Martial in the way that he dribbled and could go past players before putting the ball in the back of the net. On his day he was a ridiculous player and that showed later on when he got big moves to Chelsea and Barcelona because he was in a different stratosphere to everyone else playing in the Championship.

Colin Hendry signed when I was there and was a brilliant guy – all or nothing and a top pro. Kevin Nolan was coming through at the time and was Sam's favourite, he loved him and Michael Ricketts was just beginning to burst onto the scene, scoring a lot of goals. He ended up playing for England.

I was quite close to Hasney Aljofree and we used to have some great nights out in Manchester together with a lad called Warren Dunn and Haroon Latif and his brothers. He always reminds me of one time we were out together and I was steaming after coming out of Royales. We'd been giving it large on the spirits or 'top shelfers' as we used to call them, I think Haroon was driving that night and says he had to stop so I could get out and be sick in the middle of the road. We had some great times, Hasney was a good centre-half or midfield player and is a youth coach at United now. We still play golf together sometimes.

I also had a good relationship with Dean Holdsworth and we became good mates. He was a top striker who maybe just lacked that little bit of pace but he scored a few goals and like Big Dunc at Everton I used to set a few up for him.

## Dean Holdsworth – Bolton Wanderers 1997-2003

*He'll say that but I can't remember too many!*

*John was more than a team-mate to me and we became close friends. We spent a lot of time outside of football together discussing the game or playing golf. We had a special friendship.*

*We got on very well and really gelled with a similar sense of humour and we're still mates now. We're not in each other's pockets and I've not seen him for a long time but when we do it just clicks back together again. We've been through some fun times together and anything we did together we always managed to find a funny side to it.*

*We had a great team at Bolton and ended up getting promoted to the Premier League beating Preston in the play-off final at the Millennium stadium in Cardiff. I remember us getting called 'The Crazy Bunch' rather than 'The Crazy Gang' that I was part of at Wimbledon a few years earlier. We had a great team spirit which got us through the tough times because whenever we lost we usually bounced back very well.*

*It was a great time for the club and we were beginning to fulfil our potential and more. John was a strong part of the puzzle for quite a while, he fitted in well, always gave everything and was a good professional.*

*John's personality makes him a little more laid-back than a lot of players I've come across – he was different in that respect and maybe some of the managers he played for could have helped him a little bit differently. He's a strong personality and he probably needed someone to put his arm round him every now and then. He needed to feel loved and I'm not sure he always got that.*

Things went well the first year I was there, I was playing regularly with a good level of consistency and setting up a few goals for the forwards. I also found the back of the net myself on occasion and scored arguably the best goal of my career from 40 yards against Gillingham. It was a decent goal and got replayed a few times on Soccer AM.

I was just inside their half playing right-back and normally I would have been looking for Dean but I saw the keeper off his line and just hit it. I knew it was in as soon as I hit it, straight in the top corner and I meant it as well. It was a great goal but I've never managed to find any footage of it which is a shame.

For a defender I scored a few goals and it's one of the best feelings you can have, in training I would often play up-front in five-a-side because I was always confident I could sniff out a goal. Most of the time as soon as you hit it you know it's going in, like a golf putt. It's an indescribable feeling and if you're not a renowned goalscorer you don't really know what to do with yourself or how to celebrate. Most of the time you just get crowded by your team-mates and I feel sorry for players nowadays with VAR when you don't know if it's going to be chalked off.

We just missed out on promotion that year but reached the semi-finals of the FA Cup narrowly losing out on penalties to Aston Villa at the old Wembley. I was named on the bench that day and that allows you to take in the occasion a bit more. I came on at the beginning of extra time and played for about half an hour. I remember the pitch being tiny but it always looked huge when you saw it on TV, it felt really claustrophobic it's just the fans were further away from the pitch. It was tight.

It could sap you though, even though I didn't play for that long I still felt tired and it would have been a lot harder for the lads who started the game. You used to see players going down with cramp in the FA Cup final and I think the whole occasion can get to you but it was a good experience. It finished 0-0 after extra time so went to penalties and a few of our lads missed theirs before it got to me. We were probably very unlucky to go out like that having matched them for the duration of the game because they were a good Premier League side including the likes of Gareth Southgate, Paul Merson, Gareth Barry, Benito Carbone and Dion Dublin. If we'd have got through it would have been the last final played at that stadium before they bulldozed it but it wasn't to be.

Even if we had got there it's unlikely I would have played because I was suffering with a double hernia. I should have gone in earlier for the operation but Sam wanted me to delay it because he needed me in the first team. I was hardly training at this point but he put me in because he knew I could do a job.

We played Manchester City at Maine Road a few days after the Villa game and I was up against a lad called Mark Kennedy who was a tricky little winger made worse by the fact I couldn't run. We were 2-0 down after 25 minutes and I think they scored down my side.

I was brought off and Sam absolutely hammered me at half-time. I had a go back at him and he really didn't like that but I couldn't physically run and when I kicked the ball the pain was horrendous. It felt sickening. The next day I went in for the operation and that was me for the rest of the season.

The following year they'd brought in a few players to challenge for places and I had a few injuries so I was in and out of the team and just couldn't get my rhythm back. I started to feel unhappy again and felt that something wasn't right with me. Every club I went to after I left United followed a similar pattern. I'd turn up and ace the trial, they'd sign me and things would go well for a while but then something in my head would go and it was like there was this voice at the back of my head saying, "You don't want to be here, fuck it up for yourself."

That's when I'd press the self-destruct button and probably lean more into having a bad attitude or chip on my shoulder. I still felt I was carrying a lot of the baggage from what had happened at Everton which had left a sour taste in my mouth. I was a lot more sceptical now and starting to hate football and people in general. I knew that I'd already had a big opportunity at a massive club and it had messed up partly through my own fault and I was struggling to bounce back from it.

I can empathise with someone like Ravel Morrison. He was another one who everyone said was a ridiculous player when he was a young lad at United but ever since he's struggled to do it on any sort of consistent level. He has all the talent in the world but something in his head isn't right and it's damaged him. I don't know what's gone on in his personal life but there's something in his make-up which seems to implode at every club he goes to which is a bit like myself. With both of us there's a player in there but we're just not wired up like the ultimate professional. The pressure of dealing with whatever is going on in your personal life or your head and trying to play football at the same time can be too much. I actually met him at England headquarters a few years ago when I was doing some scouting and he seemed like a really nice lad.

The red mist was starting to descend again and I got sent-off playing against Sheffield Wednesday. One of their lads, Alan Quinn, kept raking my ankles and constantly doing me late. Mid-way through the second half I just snapped and punched him in the chest. Either the referee or the linesman saw it and that was it – straight red.

You feel guilty getting sent off and that you've let your team-mates down but at the time I was in the red zone. There was a lot of built-up frustration in me and I just exploded and lashed out. My ankles were dodgy anyway. I played in one game not long after and went over on it after going up for a header. I felt it snap and it just went under me. It came up like a balloon and I couldn't run so that was more time on the sidelines.

After that I struggled getting back in the side and I remember being sent to play in a game for the reserves away at Oldham. By this point my head had completely gone and the demons had set in. It was a horrible night and I questioned why I was even playing. There were other players in the squad who played in my position and it felt like I didn't even need to be there. My ankle had already been wrecked and the pitch was a mess. It was muddy, wet and windy and I was worried about doing further damage. I remember looking round as we were about to kick-off and just thinking, "I don't want to be here."

I'll be honest, it was the only game in my career where I sacked it off and didn't take it seriously and it showed. Everything about that night just felt wrong. I think Per Frandsen played in midfield and I remember him shouting to me, "John you need to start doing some running lad!"

I got brought off after about 20 minutes because the coaching staff knew my head wasn't right. I went straight into the dressing room and I remember Phil Brown coming in and absolutely roasting me, "You are a fucking disgrace and you will never play for this club again!"

"Good, because I don't fucking want to," was my response and that was my Bolton career pretty much done and dusted. I didn't try and work my way back into the manager's plans I just accepted it was over. I was sent to train with the kids again and just got on with it. Every player knows that feeling when you turn up for training and you just know you're not involved and out on your own so you just go through the motions.

They knew I wasn't 100% for the cause, which you have to be for Big Sam, and they wanted me out of there. I wasn't interested anymore and they knew that. There were no slanging matches or anything like that although I do remember playing for the reserves against the first team in a practice game. Me being me I turned up and made a point of playing on the wing and tearing the full-back apart. I remember Allardyce saying, "Why the fuck aren't you playing like that in my first team?"

I just shrugged my shoulders. I just wanted to be able to play with freedom but every time I was set up in a first team squad they always wanted me to play in a certain way rather than just let me go out and play. Having said that it's scandalous when I look back now how I could turn it on and off when I wanted. I was so fixated on being my own person that I cut off my nose to spite my face. It's not a good trait to have but that was how my head worked at the time. I knew I was a good player.

## Steve Robinson

*There were a few managers John didn't see eye to eye with and he had this thing about him. I wouldn't call it an arrogance but if a manager got into most players they'd be determined to prove him wrong and I don't think John had that in him. I think something in him would just stick two fingers up to them and switch off, almost like he didn't really want it. Was that his way of getting out of it? Did he want to be a footballer? I'm not sure.*

*He was that talented but did he actually want to work and do that extra bit? It's like he didn't have that will to push on. He has the persona of being really laid-back and I don't think he is but he could play football that way because he was so good.*

It all just broke down really. There were no hard feelings between me and Sam. I've seen him a few times since and we always have a chat. He knew my character and in the end we just had to part ways. It was an amicable thing. It was very business-like because we both knew how football worked. He's a good manager who is seen as old fashioned but is really quite technical. Half the time he didn't have the players to do what he wanted to do or play attractive football. It was a shame what happened with England because it was his dream job but he messed up.

The club ended up getting promoted that year by beating Preston in the play-off final. It was another missed opportunity in my career where I could have kicked on or been part of something. Bolton became a very good Premier League side for a decade after I left but I never looked at them in the same way as I did with United and wondered whether I could have been a part of it. My association with the club ended when I left. While they were celebrating the promotion and preparing for life in the Premier League I was heading for the seaside.

# BOMB SQUAD

**D**RIVING HOME AFTER A GAME I BURST into tears. It had all got too much. I was the captain of Blackpool Football Club and I'd just played in a game where I'd been booed by my own fans.

We were struggling as a team near the bottom of the league. We were losing and as skipper I was deemed to be one of the better players, but my laid-back persona isn't a good thing from the fans' point of view when things aren't going well. To them it probably looked like I wasn't bothered and in truth by this point my head was all over the place anyway.

I could hear the jeering growing in the crowd every time I was on the ball. To any player being booed by your own fans is the ultimate insult and you could hear them all, "O'Kane you're shit. Get back to United you fucking reject!"

It stirred something in me and it got my back up. Usually when you're having a bad time you don't want the ball but that day I was the complete opposite. I was playing right-back but that didn't really matter to me, I kept taking the ball in stupid positions and demanding it again, "Give me the ball, give me the fucking ball!"

I kept receiving it, taking players on trying to make things happen and I remember pinging a ball 50 or 60 yards over the full-backs head and I think we nearly scored from it. I turned to one of the people in the crowd who'd been giving it to me: "Is that alright for you mate? You keep booing, want to come have a go instead?"

Having a go back is the worst thing you can do in that situation but it was partly tongue in cheek and shows where my head was at the time. Sat in the car on the way home, I was upset because my pride had been hurt and I did care but I was sat there sobbing just thinking, "What am I doing? I don't need this." All the pressure and anxiety had just become too much.

It was a low point and showed something wasn't right with me. I was breaking down inside and struggling to cope with it all – the stress, the tics and the pressure of playing. When you feel like you're getting beaten down all the time it can be harder to get back up. I just felt like I was getting battered all the time and I just couldn't take it anymore.

I was damaged from the experiences I'd had at Everton and Bolton where I'd seen the cynical side of the game and was losing my love for it. I knew I was good enough but something in me just didn't want to conform to the system because I didn't feel comfortable in it. I was fixated on being my own person and had become disillusioned with the regimented lifestyle, it just felt like I was always battling something - ultimately it was exhausting.

The two sides of my head were going to war with each other and the guy who didn't want to be part of that regime was winning and starting to take over. The part of me that loved the game and wanted to do well was getting smaller and smaller as I seriously questioned for the first time whether I needed this anymore.

I was struggling big time but I just had to get on with it. The next day I just carried on like normal, the end was coming though.

I'd turned up at Blackpool because it was another contract. Andy Bower came with me to the meeting when I went to sign for the club and we met Steve McMahon. He was keen to bring me to the club for a new challenge, he was a bit of ball player and man-management wise seemed top drawer.

I remember going to Bloomfield Road and at the time it was undergoing redevelopment so they virtually had half a ground. The Blackpool FC sign was hanging off and the place looked like it had seen better days. With the ground being so close to the seafront as well it was so cold and windy, it always seemed to be constantly gusting with wind coming straight off the Irish Sea and the training ground near the airport was exactly the same.

### Andy Bower

*I remember turning up outside the ground and they'd knocked two sides of it down. I remember looking at the sign for Blackpool Football Club and the 'P' had fallen off and it was covered in seagull shit.*

*Steve McMahon invited us in and I remember walking round Bloomfield Road as he gave us a tour. We're leaning against the barrier overlooking the pitch, it's summer, there's two stands missing and it's absolutely freezing.*

*McMahon's trying to sell the club to John, saying he wants to build a team around him and that he wanted to sign him when he was manager of Swindon. I could see John's face and he's probably thinking he's come from United, Everton, Bolton and now to this. McMahon's giving it all this spiel, "What do you want John? What can I do to make you sign for me?"*

*I jokingly just said, "Give him the number four shirt and the captaincy…"*

*"Done."*

*He won't admit it but that was how John ended up captain of Blackpool. We had a good laugh there and he was quality in his first season. Head and shoulders above.*

Pre-season used to be running up the sand dunes on the beach and I used to enjoy the training because more or less all we used to do was five-a-sides, which I loved. McMahon had been a baller at Liverpool, he used to love himself a little bit but could still play to be fair and I really liked him at first.

You could tell he'd been a top player and I remember him bringing Kenny Dalglish to training once and everyone was buzzing. Once he joined in though it was disappointing because he couldn't really play or run anymore. He must have been in his early fifties by that point and it was a bit sad really. He couldn't really move.

We had a good environment and there was a really good camaraderie about the squad. It was a really tight group and we had some good nights out in Blackpool. There was a really good bond and atmosphere.

We had some decent players like Paul Simpson, Martin Bullock and Brett Ormerod, some good lads and technical players. Steve McMahon liked to play football and I think he got everything he could out of that team. Tommy Jaszczun played left-back and our goalkeeper Phil Barnes was a decent keeper but used to get it quite a lot from the manager.

Ian Marshall was there, he was a great guy; an old school player who wouldn't take any shit. He could play in a few different positions and had played for Oldham earlier in his career in the Premier League. On his day he was a brilliant player and deceptively quick, he was a bit of a tramp but a very funny guy.

I used to room with Richie Wellens on away trips and we got on really well. He was a few years below me at United and a bit of a Tom Cleverley sort of player who had a very good career in the Football League before moving into management. He liked a laugh too did Wellens, he once taped an extra 'C' onto the back of my shirt before a game to go at the front of my name. I ran out of the tunnel for a game completely unaware of the amusement of the crowd – he got fined by the FA for it.

Just as at Everton and Bolton, things went really well at first. I was made captain and played about 50 games in a few different positions in my first season. We got to the LDV Vans Trophy final at the Millennium stadium in Cardiff which was a massive game to play in. It was a big occasion for the club with a lot of fans there. We played really well on the day and beat Cambridge United 4-1 with Martin Bullock having a really good game. It was a great achievement for the club to win a trophy, I've still got the medal now and I'm proud of it. It was a big deal to win in those days before it took its current form with Premier League under-23s sides being allowed to play in it.

There were some good times on and off the pitch. I remember a few of us got to turn on Blackpool Illuminations one year which was a surreal experience, they probably couldn't get someone from Coronation Street to do it so just made do with us. It was quality when I look back on it. My auntie and uncle used to live in Blackpool so as a kid we'd be there every summer and I have lots of good memories of the place.

The club seemed like a decent set-up and you could see what they were trying to do. The owners, the Oyston family, aren't popular in Blackpool at all but I tried not to get involved with any of that. The fans hated them though.

It was fine until McMahon started trying to bully some of the other lads when things weren't going well. I stood up to him a few times and he just couldn't handle it so there started to be a bit of needle between us. I remember him elbowing me once in a five-a-side so I returned the favour and went through him. I could tell that he didn't like it that I'd got him back and we started to clash more regularly.

I started the 2002/03 season in the team but often found myself dropped to the bench. I'd started to switch off already because there were players being picked ahead of me who I didn't really think should be playing. The manager wasn't picking players who were technically good, he must have just seen a different kind of player he wanted in there. He knew my character and recognised that my attitude wasn't spot on and in fairness to him he was right because my head was beginning to unravel again.

He didn't help himself though and seemed to have it in for me. I remember us getting battered 5-0 playing away somewhere but I'd been sat on the bench all game. Even though I didn't play he tried to blame me for it because I'd not warmed up enough. They had us in to watch the video the next day at the training ground and I was sat at the back of the room with Richie Wellens. I remember McMahon stood at the front when he was going through the tape saying: "And O'Kane, I know he didn't play but just didn't want to come on or get warmed up."

"If you wanted me to come on, shouldn't you have been telling me to get warmed up, gaffer?" I bit back.

The whole squad was sat there and you could tell he didn't know what to do, so he decided to go personal.

"Where are you going to be in ten years' time? I'll tell you where you're going to be. You're going to be working in a fucking shop, doing nothing."

"Nah I'll be retired by then. I'll decide where I'm going to be and what I'm going to do. Don't worry."

He was getting redder and redder. Wellens and the other lads were tapping me to get me to stop. It was funny because he'd tried to get personal with me in front of the rest of the squad and couldn't handle it when I gave a bit back. I was a grown man by then and in a weird way I liked the confrontation and wasn't going to shy away from it. A lot of the time, to get anywhere in football, you have to just take it on the chin but I just couldn't do it. I couldn't conform and was stubborn because I wasn't going to take anybody belittling me.

### Richie Wellens – Blackpool 2000-05

*I'd known John when we were both at United and I was in the 'A' and 'B' teams whilst he was in the reserves.*

*We trained together a lot and he was a very laid-back character but very talented. He was very composed and technically he was good off both feet. I think he would admit that at a young age he probably wasn't guided the right way and his attitude maybe lacked a bit to make a first team player at a club the size of Manchester United, but from there he got a good move to Everton.*

*I got to know him better when he signed for Blackpool and we used to room together on away trips. We were both pretty similar and had come from a good football club. We used to socialise together and go out for meals.*

*I think he was dealt with very harshly at Blackpool and his personality clashed with the management. John's a very laid-back person who doesn't take too well to straight up or unconstructive criticism and Steve McMahon was the total opposite so they were at loggerheads.*

*I think it was probably the wrong move for him at the wrong time. When you've got a personality like John you need to pick the right manager rather than the club to get the best out of him but by that point if I'm being honest I think his passion and love for the game had started to ebb away.*

I loved playing football as a kid and the freedom it brought but as soon as the rules and structure came in I couldn't handle it. Being told what to do all the time and spoken down to wasn't in my make-up and I just wanted to rebel against it.

I couldn't seem to hold a relationship with certain managers who didn't get me but I'd give anything for the right manager like Stan Ternent or Howard Kendall earlier in my career. If I liked them I'd do anything for them and run through a brick wall, if I didn't I'd subconsciously sabotage myself so I didn't help them out which is messed up really when you think about it but something in me would refuse to be in that environment.

Some managers don't understand that players are just people at the end of the day. Some need an arm around them and others you need to get into a bit more. A lot of managers can't seem to grasp it. If players don't conform to them they just isolate them and get rid. It's part of the reason why top players often don't make good managers because they can't deal with players who don't meet their very high standards and don't have the personal skills to understand them. A good manager needs the personal side as well and to understand that everyone has a different make-up.

There's a lot of stuff that goes on behind the scenes that the fans don't see and by the New Year I was out of the first team picture altogether. I could feel the cycle that I'd gone through at Everton and Bolton happening again and I knew that something had to change.

The manager began to treat me like I didn't exist and I was made to train away from the rest of the lads with the 'Bomb Squad'. A 'Bomb Squad' in football terms is a group of players that the manager just isn't interested in and is often made to train separate from the rest of the squad. There's one at every club and at that time at Blackpool there were quite a few of us including myself, Jamie Milligan and Graham Fenton who were desperate to get out of the club.

It tended to be the players who weren't playing in the team and were on half-decent contracts having come from bigger clubs. There's always politics involved as well, managers are sometimes told to get rid of players who are on decent money and draining the club in the eyes of the owners, especially if they're not playing.

It comes from the top so it probably just wasn't down to Steve McMahon. If he'd been told that he needed to get us out of the club he'd have had to find a way to do that which in this case was to treat us like shit and make us do endless amounts of running to break us.

On a Saturday morning while the squad were preparing for the game that afternoon, we'd have to go in and train where they'd run us until we literally couldn't move anymore. They made us come in on a Sunday and just made us run, to try and piss us off and make us leave. It was torture in a way, they just wanted to punish us.

I still had time to run on my contract and could see what was going on so would do just enough to get through it, I'd complete it but I wasn't going to bust a gut. Some of the other lads like Jamie Milligan would want to work on his fitness for himself but I wasn't bothered. He was a good player who had been at Everton with me and he could rip it up but McMahon picked his son ahead of him. The assistant manager, Mark Seagraves, used to take us and wouldn't say a word to us apart from: "Right, on the line, ready – GO!"

And that would be it.

Imagine going into your day job and your boss telling you that instead of using a pen today they're going to make you use a pencil or taking your chair away and making you stand. That's what it was like, just little things that you would do to a kid who had misbehaved at school.

I was 28 by this point and knew mentally it wasn't good for me. After a while I just thought: "I don't need this." My character was changing and I was becoming angrier, nastier and more bitter. That came across as almost wanting the team to lose even though they were my mates because it would hurt the manager and the club. I didn't want to be like that anymore.

## Ben Thornley – Blackpool 2002-03

*Mine and John's paths crossed again later in our careers when I signed for Blackpool. I didn't want to be so far away from home and not involved at Aberdeen, which at the time was the way it was going, so it was a move back closer to home for me.*

*I remember being sat in the changing room before training and John walking in and he was as surprised as I was to see him. It's always pleasing to see a familiar face when you're new at a club because you always have a bit of self-doubt and anticipation.*

*I was looking forward to playing with him again but it very quickly became apparent that he was being overlooked by the manager. I remember there being a few lads there who were desperate to get out of Blackpool and maybe John was feeling that as well because there's nothing worse than training all week knowing that you won't be picked in the team on a Saturday no matter what you do.*

*It's a hard place to be in football and that's one aspect of it that people on the outside don't see. There's a perception of football being really glamorous with a brilliant lifestyle but it can be a very lonely, dark place when things aren't going well for you and I think John at that time was not far off being there.*

I made a one-off appearance for the first team on 26th April 2003 in a 3-0 defeat at Cheltenham Town. They must have been short, I have absolutely no recollection of it. That ended up being my last game in professional football.

I remember going into a meeting with McMahon not long after, he called me into his office and said: "Have you changed your mind about leaving yet?"

"Erm, yeah. Just pay me up, we're done aren't we?" And that was it. I shook hands with him and walked out. It had all gone very sour but I don't hate him. I actually liked him when I first joined because he was funny and he would have a bit of a joke with the lads. He was a character and he had probably been told he had to get rid of me. My only problem with him was the way he went about it. I'd have respected him a lot more if he'd have to come to me and just said, "Look John, I can't keep you, we need to let you go." If he'd have tackled it head-on like that and spoken to me like a man I would have taken it a lot better. But it's the way he tried to force me out of the club that rubbed me up the wrong way and said a lot about him as a manager.

I was 28 and should have been at my peak but I'd had enough. Football can sour very quickly and there's probably thousands of stories out there that are similar to mine. I knew it was time to burst the whole football bubble that

I'd lived in for half of my life and try to make a go of it in the real world.

I could have got another club but I had no desire to because I would have just been repeating the same cycle as what had happened with my last three teams. I didn't want to go on trial and put myself through it all again. I've no idea if any clubs were interested in signing me because I never looked and I wasn't bothered.

A lot of footballers become almost institutionalised and will do anything to stay in the game but I knew I had to get out. Some players go on for as long as they can and struggle when they retire but in the end I couldn't wait to leave it behind and I just faded into the background.

Accepting I was finished was a massive relief. I felt free for the first time in years but once that had worn off I had to decide what I was going to do for the rest of my life.

# THE PRIDE OF HYDE

MY OLD PAL DAVID BECKHAM SIGNED for Real Madrid in the summer of 2003 whilst I was done with football. It's crazy how things can work out.

I decided to move back to Nottingham and in with Robbo whilst I worked out what I was going to do next. I felt free with no pressure and just felt relief but now I needed a job. I'd just got a nice little pay-off from Blackpool but knew that wasn't going to last forever and I had no qualifications. Reality hit home.

I looked at going down the coaching route and remember trying to go for one of my badges which was just a two-week rigmarole and mind numbing so I didn't have the patience for it. I thought about doing a bit of property because there was a boom in the market around that time and I ended up buying a couple, one of which my mum ended up living in when she moved back to Nottingham but nothing really came of it.

Then one day I got a call from Tony Ellis who'd had a decent career playing for the likes of Preston North End, Blackpool and Bury - he was now assistant manager at Hyde United. He'd heard that I'd sort of retired and asked if I was interested in going to play a few games for them in non-league.

I'd never heard of the club or even which league they were in but the deal was that I didn't really have to train, maybe once a week if that, and just come up for the games and go back to Nottingham. They offered me about £300 a game cash in hand and said they'd make me captain.

As far as I was concerned if I never played football again when I left Blackpool, I would have been fine with that but the whole arrangement sounded ideal and when I went up there something in my mind just clicked and I was like, "Right, let's fucking do this."

It was a quality club and I loved it. There were loads of people behind the scenes who helped out to keep the place running and you got to know all the kit-men and ground staff personally. Fans of Premier League teams often don't realise how these smaller clubs have a real sense of spirit and community. There was a real connection with the fans and you had a close relationship with them because you could hear everything when you were playing and you would be in the bar with the supporters after the game.

Hyde were well-run and were getting some good players in who could have easily been playing at a higher level. Jamie Milligan came after he'd been released by Blackpool himself and used it as a springboard to get back up the leagues because he ended up going to Fleetwood Town where he became a club legend. There were guys like Phil Salt and Neil Tolson there and Tony Ellis was still playing a bit when I got there, so they were a good footballing team.

Steve Waywell was the manager and knew the non-league scene inside out. He was quite successful at that level which isn't easy because you've got to be able to attract players and a lot of them are juggling their day jobs alongside training, playing and all the travelling across the North of England to places like Workington, Blyth Spartans and Spennymoor.

Most of the lads would turn up for training or to play

having just done a full day shift. Some of them would still be in their work gear and it was real life. We'd only really train once a week, usually on a Tuesday, and you'd really only have about an hour and a half on the pitch because we had to pay for it, so it was difficult to do anything tactical or shape work but we had a good set of technical players. The club had a link with City because it's that side of Manchester and City used to play their reserve games at our ground Ewen Fields. I remember playing against their lads a few times and we held our own.

I didn't really know what to expect of the standard, they wanted me to play at centre-half which is where I'd always wanted to play, and run the show. Me being me I wanted to play midfield and attack but I remember trying it and I just couldn't believe how fast the game was and how little space you had with players knowing I was ex-United and trying to snap me.

So I found a home at centre-back and I loved playing there. There were a few difficult games but I found it easy from there because I could just read everything in front of me as I had when I was younger. I just wish I'd had more chance to play there during my professional career but there are other things you have to consider like height and maybe I ended up being a couple of inches too short.

The fans took to me straight away and I just felt really comfortable playing for them. Hyde was the place where I got my passion for football back because it was the happiest I'd been in the game since my first season at Everton under Howard Kendall or maybe some of the moments from my early days with Blackpool. I just felt free like I had been on the streets of Bilborough as a kid in Nottingham.

There wasn't as much pressure as there is at higher levels and the crowds were smaller but I still had to perform. I'd been searching for that freedom and I was playing football for enjoyment again, rather than just a job. The money was half-decent but it wasn't about that. I felt mentally strong enough to cope with playing again which allowed me to break the cycle that I'd been through at Everton, Bolton and Blackpool of fallouts with managers and self-destruction.

The games came thick and fast too, it was pretty much a couple of games a week and I was getting job satisfaction from playing in them. It all just clicked because I was happy in my life physically and mentally.

I loved being captain because I'd always known that was in me, it just needed the right environment to bring it out. A lot of people over the course of my career didn't see that because I was so laid-back but I knew I could man-manage players on and off the pitch. I could give it a bit of needle if the game required but if I saw a player struggling I'd just have a bit of a joke with them to calm them down.

Sometimes you need to know which players need a kick up the backside, like I often did, or those that need a bit more of an arm around them. I knew what it took but when you get labelled 'Spaceman' or lazy it sticks with you and people dismiss you as any sort of leader but I went to Hyde and led the team and we were very successful in the time I was there.

We won the double-double in the first two years I was there with back-to-back promotions and league cups to be promoted to the Conference North which is hard to do, even at that level, but we had a great group. It was a great time for the club and we just came from nowhere, a bit like Salford City but with no real financial backing.

I had a couple of offers to go back full-time and play in the Football League again but I never followed it up and I didn't have an agent by that stage. There would have been scouts watching us but I think they knew with me it was a waste of time pursuing it. There was always my history as well which probably put a few clubs off and in any case I'd moved on by that stage.

Things went really well until I snapped my Achilles in one of the first games of the season after we'd been promoted to the Conference North. At first when it happened I thought someone had kicked me from behind when I'd run onto the ball but then I just collapsed.

I'd never felt anything like it before so didn't know what it was. They rushed me off to hospital in an ambulance and it kept me out for pretty much the rest of the season. I did come back for the last few games when they tried to rush me back for the run-in but I knew it wasn't right.

I came on as a sub in my first game back and remember putting in a massive sliding tackle and feeling really good. I played a few games but there was always a worry in the back of my mind that it would happen again. It just didn't feel 100% when I ran and I didn't have faith in it to hold up. An injury like that can impact you mentally too and I couldn't really go all out in training. I remember running around the pitch when they were trying to get me fit and just hobbling. The club needed to get a few players off the wage bill and by that point I thought I'd done my bit. I had a chat with the manager and I think he knew my heart wasn't in it anymore.

I was 31 by then and I'd be going out on much better terms than if I'd stopped completely after Blackpool. I'd had a great time at Hyde and played well over a hundred games for them which is a lot if you consider I was injured for most of the last season I was there. I was still young but felt the time was right to call it a day and by this stage I had other things going on in my life. I'd just become a father.

I'd met my partner Simone on a night out in Manchester. She'd spotted me in The Living Room earlier on and then we'd gone round the corner to a nightclub which wouldn't let us in. I made a point of standing next to her in the queue and she helped get me in. Once we'd got inside she kicked me up the backside and just said, "Any chance of buying us a drink seeing as I got you in!"

I was still living in Nottingham and I remember for a few days after thinking that I liked her but couldn't remember what she looked like but I decided to ring her anyway and see if she wanted to come over for a night out. She had the balls to do it and came down. I went to meet her with Robbo at the train station and was panicking a little bit because I was literally meeting a stranger but she came over and gave me a hug and that was it really. We got on really well and we just clicked.

She was still at university and we had some great times in our early days together. I eventually moved back up to Stockport to live with my step-dad's sister for a while and Simone ended up moving in with me there. Six months down the line she fell pregnant with my eldest son Taelor so we had to make a decision. She was from Darwen in Lancashire so I agreed to buy a house there so I could look after the baby while she continued her studying.

When Taelor was born I was still hobbling round with my foot in a big boot after my Achilles operation so looking after a baby whilst Simone was at uni was tough. It's not the easiest task at the best of times especially when I couldn't walk. I enjoyed it though and had a few months out to let my foot heal properly.

Now I knew there wouldn't be any more football it was time to get a proper job. I remember asking a local roofer in the pub if he needed anyone to help him out and he agreed to take me on as his labourer. I was quite strong and my foot had healed by then. It was summer when I started so the weather was good, we had our tops off working in the sun and had a good laugh. The guy I was working with was quite a big bloke and I remember him putting his foot through a few of them which was funny once we knew he was alright. We had some good times to be fair.

I enjoyed it and it's weird to stand on the roof of a house, I felt quite powerful in a way when I was up there. It was proper graft but I've never had any issues with heights. I remember doing a bungee jump in Ayia Napa over some rocks with Robbo and Goughy. It's easy enough to walk on a roof, the main part is just not to look down.

It's not an easy job though, everything has to be spot on or it's no good. After being stuck in that repetitive cycle in football it felt great just to be out there doing something for myself and I'll always be grateful to him for giving me my first job.

I ended up going into business with one of the lads from Hyde – Phil Salt. He was a roofer by trade so we bought a van and cracked on with it. We went 50/50, in fairness he did most of the work but I would carry all the stuff up to him. It was a good workout and the banter on building sites is always brilliant.

I worked for a scaffolder for a bit on good money but it was a bit less enjoyable in winter and I knew that was enough for me. It was the only time in my life where after a day's work I actually wanted a pint and it makes you understand why a lot of tradesman go to the pub before they go home. In a weird way you need it just to wind down.

I enjoyed roofing and the physical side of it but I knew mentally that I needed a challenge. It didn't feel like something I could do for another 30 years or more and I knew I was destined for something so I moved on.

I didn't find what it was straight away though. I used to help out Simone's mum and dad working in a corner shop they owned and I managed to blag myself a job in an office for a finance company in Manchester. I worked in the post room sorting out all the mail and I remember getting the train in every day with my suit on absolutely buzzing that I'd got myself a job in the big city.

It was fine for a while but I started to feel a little bit disrespected by some of the other members of staff there. They'd have me taking sandwiches and coffee into the meeting room for the important guys and they all looked down on me and not one said thank you.

I remember giving one of them the wrong post one day and they just threw it back at me. I've always treated people how they treat me. In society you often get bosses who treat you like shit and I just couldn't stand for it. I was there about five or six months and sort of knew it wasn't for me, I just enjoyed going into Manchester like a working man.

I'd tried a few different things by this point but everybody has that thing in life that they're meant to do. I was about to find mine and it would surprise a few people.

# BEST JOB IN THE WORLD

I WAS SAT AT HOME ONE DAY WHEN ONE OF Simone's mates Charlotte asked me what I was up to. I was looking for a new opportunity and she was a lead manager for a care group looking after vulnerable kids. She suggested it because there was a house in Preston that were looking for people.

Charlotte got me an interview and so I turned up all smart in my suit. A lad called Jamie interviewed me, I said all the right things and that I was a patient guy who needed a new challenge.

I got the job. I wasn't too sure what I'd let myself in for, a lot of the kids there had had a tough time and were vulnerable. One side of the place was a care facility whilst the other part provided teaching for kids who weren't able to attend normal comprehensive schools.

## Jamie Farrell – Former Colleague

*It's not every day you interview a former footballer and I knew who John was. It must be quite a rare thing for ex-players to go into when they retire but he was a lovely guy to work with, good fun and passionate about his job.*

*He was good at it too. I remember we took the kids to a Blackpool legends game at Chorley, some of the fans recognised John and came over to speak to him. He dealt with it all really well whilst making sure the kids he was looking after were safe and happy. A brilliant guy.*

For my first day I made the mistake of wearing my Nike golf jumper which I loved and cost about £50. It got ripped to shreds.

I had training on how to deal with different situations. Some of which were very challenging but you have to put up a front, show you're not scared and just deal with it. A bit like in football I guess.

I remember there was one lad that if you got too close to him he'd grab you and take you to the floor because of some horrible stuff he'd seen as a kid. He was a lovely lad and you could just be talking to him fine and then suddenly that instinct in him would kick in. Another would soil himself and throw it at you. Some kids would be two-to-one so you'd have to have two adults with them at any one time. There were kids there who were autistic and if you were taking them out in the minibus you had to drive on a set route.

It was a challenge and in a weird way it was like a drug that kept you going back for more. It's what I'd always wanted, a job that got me out of bed every day where I knew I was helping somebody and I loved it. Football was never really a challenge to me, it was just going through the same regimented routine. With working in care, every single day was different.

You didn't know what you were going to turn up to or which kids you were going to be working with. There were a good bunch of adults who you worked with on a daily basis and we were all in the same boat. They knew that I'd played football but they didn't care who I was. You'd just get on with your job, I'd be wiping backsides and sleeping over on 18-hour night-shifts so I could be there for a few days straight and you could be up all night if things kicked off.

Eventually I moved over to the teaching side of it where the hours suited me a bit better because I had a young family. A lad called Daniel Waterhouse wanted to put me through all my NVQs and knew I could deal with it so I'd help out teaching in the classrooms.

We'd do short lessons with the kids and then take them on days out. That still had its challenges as you'd get kids who didn't want to do the work and just destroy the classroom. After you've done a job like that, nothing can faze you because you've seen hell in a way and had to deal with it.

It was rewarding though and the job satisfaction was good. It was hard work but with me having my own mental health issues I felt comfortable being around those kids because I could relate to some of what they had to go through.

## Daniel Waterhouse – Former Colleague

*I worked with John for about three years. He was a great guy to have around and you could tell that he'd had a good upbringing at United. He understood people and was like the glue that held the team together. When there were difficult days he was always there with a joke or something to lift people and make them laugh.*

*I'm a Burnley fan, so I remember John playing for us on loan and he got dog's abuse! We used to do a session on a Thursday morning at Edge Hill University where we used football as a vehicle to teach the kids social rules. It taught them things like turn-taking, teamwork and applauding and valuing each other as people. John was integral to that with his professional background and added a lot of value to it.*

*He could do things that the kids would be impressed with and they looked up to him. There were kids from different backgrounds who faced certain challenges and John really went above and beyond to connect with them, putting their needs first. A brilliant guy and he's one of my mates.*

In that industry you often find yourself moving on to other projects after a while and I fancied going into schools. I worked in a college with a special needs class in the art room which was great because I'd always loved drawing.

I worked in quite a few schools where I'd go in to help kids who'd been mistreated or had learning disabilities like autism. A lot of kids these days are on the spectrum, some of them probably don't even know it but when you've worked in that kind of environment it's easier to spot in people. It's the same with adults too, it's like a sixth sense you get from working in that kind of job and being on the spectrum myself. It can only be a positive that awareness around it has grown in recent years so there is more support available.

The trend with these placements is that they last for about 6 to 12 months and then due to issues with funding they can't keep you and the agency move you on. I used to do one-to-one supervision for a company as respite for families. I worked with a Polish lad called Marek for about a year and his was a particularly sad story. He'd come to the UK to work for his uncle who enslaved him and made him work ridiculous hours. Thankfully the police rescued him in the end. He got his own place and I used to come and take him all over Accrington on trips out. He ended up coming to my wedding and got up during the speeches and started talking about me. He brought the house down and a lot of people were in tears. It was an emotional moment and showed the value of what I was doing.

It felt like I was giving something back to society. For a former professional footballer who couldn't shake the tag of being lazy it's probably the last thing people would have expected me to go into. When you've got to restrain people, the professionalism you've got to show is on another level. You have to go above and beyond to help these kids and try and give them a little bit of happiness and dignity.

It's a unique kind of person who goes into that industry and the pay is one of the lowest in society. It's zero hours too, so if you don't work you don't get paid and the government just shun it time and time again. There's no stability and you often don't know where you're going to be from one year to the next.

There was a bit of a stigma around being an ex-footballer as well, even though I'd always wanted to just go out and work. The amount of times people found out and asked me, "Why are you doing this?"

My answer was always the same: "Why shouldn't I be doing this? I've got another 40 or 50 years of my life where I need to do something. Why shouldn't I work here?"

Football used to come up from time to time. I never brought it up myself but people would find out or remember me. Obviously on your CV you have to put your job history and the words 'Professional Footballer' would always invite a few questions:

"Who did you play for?"

"United."

"Oh really! What's Beckham like? What's Cantona like?"

It can get to be a benefit sometimes and help get you in the door but you obviously have to be able to converse and know what you're doing. Once people get bored of asking questions about United you've got to show you're competent at your job. I'd deal with the inevitable questions and after a while, once people got to know me, they saw that I was just normal like them. I felt like I could show there was more to me than someone who used to play football for a living, which a lot of players can't. A lot of them are quite bland with not a lot behind them and when they finish playing they go into coaching. It's all they know and it's their life. I knew when I was playing that there was something more I had to do and that turned out to be the care work.

I've dabbled in football since I retired. I did some coaching at Chorley with the under-18s which I really enjoyed. I know Ben Howard who's an academy coach at Blackburn and my son was there for a bit of training. He asked me to come and help him out doing a bit of part-time work at Chorley.

Ben was the coach whilst I was the motivator. Coaches need that sidekick and I think it's a role that suited me because I could see things that others couldn't. When I was training I would sometimes miss a few runs or not go quite up to the line – I could see every little short-cut like nipping inside a cone on a running drill because I'd done it myself.

I could spot the little things like substitutions and who needs to play in what position. I can see players when they're hurting and need geeing up. You've got to understand people and what makes them tick, which is something you get from working in care and football.

I enjoyed my time there but in the end I decided to call it a day because I knew with the way that times have changed I wouldn't be able to use the tools I needed to get the best out of them. I knew I might have a go at them one day and young players these days can't handle the type of bollockings that we used to get back in the day off Eric Harrison.

I knew I wouldn't be able to coach them being nice. Kids these days are a different breed and I know I couldn't work at an academy. If another opportunity came up in the future I'd consider giving it another go. It's the badges that put a lot of players off because it takes ages and having the time is another thing.

I've played a little bit myself over the last 10-15 years. I did a bit locally for a team in Darwen called Revidge Allstars with a few mates. We played five-a-side and I went in net but if we were getting beat I used to come out and score a few goals. I ended up being the highest goalscorer for the team playing in net which was funny.

It was a good laugh with some good lads who will kill me if I don't mention them. A lad called JP was player-manager, terrible player though. Luke Alemanno is a good friend who lives near me and has helped me out a lot in the last ten years. Andy Morris is another close pal who played on the team and gets me and my personality. They still go on about the time I got chipped playing in net in five-a-side goals!

I met up with the rest of the Class of '92 lads for the making of the film. We all had a kick-about at the Cliff on one of the pitches we used to call Wembley and I enjoyed being out there with the guys again. You meet up and you just crack on with it, it's like you were still in the changing room just a day ago. Nothing really changes.

I did play for the Class of '92 and friends against the Salford City first team in 2014 when they'd just bought the club, there were a few celebrities involved too. My lad Taelor got to warm up with Jack Whitehall and said he was great, he's not a bad footballer actually. Michael Vaughan was involved, so was my old mate from digs Raphael Burke.

I started the game at right-back and then moved into

midfield because we were a bit short there and just had Scholes, Butt and Giggs which isn't bad but we needed an extra body and I wanted to play with them again so I shoved Phil Neville to right-back and was in my element.

We ended up losing 5-1 – they battered us. I had forgotten how fit you needed to be and we just couldn't get near them. We started well, trying to pass it and there was a bit of needle in the game to be fair. I remember crunching someone and Butty and Scholesy giving it a bit but in the end it was like chasing shadows.

It got worse when their keeper kicked it and I went up to control it and chest it down. I was about to shoot when I just collapsed. My other Achilles had snapped to the one I did at Hyde and I knew straight away. I hobbled off and was sat next to Rio Ferdinand on the bench knowing that that was me done, possibly forever.

Phil Neville asked me in the changing room afterwards whilst I was waiting to go to hospital if I could play for United legends against Bayern Munich away at the Allianz Arena. I'm no legend but they were short of a few players and said it would be nice if I could go along.

It was the weekend after and I hoped it was just a sprain but I knew really that I'd snapped it. I kept trying to move it and it wasn't happening. I went to hospital where they confirmed it was snapped and that was the end of my Manchester United legends trip. It would have been great to go but with my luck the timing was terrible and I was gutted. I think they were going to Australia soon after as well but it wasn't happening.

I played again in 2017 in a reunion game we had for Pheasant Colts, it was good to see all the lads from our team and most of the parents turned up to watch just like the old days. I tried to play outfield but both my Achilles

were so tight that I ended up going in goal. I knew that
if it went I'd be in trouble so it's not really worth the risk
anymore. I know I could play again if I wanted to but it's
also a mental thing, the one I did at Hyde was operated on
whilst the one I did in the Salford game was just allowed to
heal naturally. I've no faith in it and just feel like it would
go again. I sometimes do a bit of training with my lads but
can't go all out so I just take it easy.

Simone and I got married in 2013. We'd been engaged for
ten years and it was a great day. A lot of emotions came out
and I cried a lot. I'd never really cried that much before
and it was embarrassing really. I went as soon as I saw her
walking down the aisle and I was struggling to get my
vows out. It's just the pressure of the day and all the build-
up got to me.

We've got three great kids and thankfully none of them
seem to have inherited my tics or twitches. They've got
all our best bits with my sporting ability coupled with
Simone's work ethic. They all work hard and I'm very
proud of them all.

My eldest Taelor is a good kid and a sensible lad.
He's a decent footballer with good technical ability and
has recently earned a youth scholarship with AFC Fylde
which is a great opportunity for him to continue his
education alongside playing full-time football. He's done
it organically having not really been on the academy scene
and I'm super proud of him for keeping going, knowing
his dad was an ex-pro and the pressure he must have felt
with that but if he's going to make it, he'll do it his own
way. He's got a brain too. I look at some of his work and it's
outstanding. Academically he's brilliant and teachers always

say his attitude is really good. He's definitely got Simone's drive.

As does my daughter Ruby who's a machine as well. She's a very good gymnast, the best in her school and you can tell that she's the O'Kane. She's got the nowty side that's been developed and passed down through generations. She's like a reincarnation of my mum which I love to see.

My youngest lad Vinny is obsessed with football. He'll come home and put a kit on straight away and looks like he might need an academy because he's got so much energy. He just wants to play all the time, in the house or outside and I have to sit him down sometimes because he's so lively.

I've always been there for my kids and always will be. I've never been the sort of dad who works long hours and then goes to the pub all evening. It's another thing which puts me off going into coaching which is more than a full-time job and I know people involved in the game who've missed out on large parts of their kids growing up. I've been lucky enough to see all mine play football, go to gymnastics or do the school run and I enjoy doing that.

I've got quite a small extended family. My Uncle Jim and his wife Sze live in Nottingham and my mum's sisters live in Bournemouth and Australia. I'm closest to my uncle, he's quite a big Forest fan and is in his seventies now. He had triplets in his fifties so I also have three younger cousins – Jack, Megan and Josh. I probably see him once a year, we're close when we need to be and all help each other out.

That definitely helped when my mum passed away in 2018 after a long battle with cancer. I'd been going with her for the treatment and appointments and you could see there was a dramatic decline in her. She was a strong lady and she battled until the end. We're both realists and I remember her telling me one day in the car she was going to die. It was a weird conversation really because we were both very matter of fact about it. We went in to see the doctors and they confirmed it. She only had a few weeks to live and even then I didn't cry. We just both sort of accepted it and I just felt numb but inside I was devastated.

I'd just picked the kids up from school knowing the end was coming when I went to see her. My Auntie Maureen had come up all the way from Dorset, she was a big help in those final weeks and I remember us sat there. I told her I'd just nip home, get a shower, get changed and come back. When I left one of the last things I said to her was, "Mum you need to let go. You've done everything for us and been brilliant. We love you." When I got home I got a call to say she'd passed away.

I went back and said my goodbyes. It was sad but in those final weeks you could just see that it wasn't her anymore. I was thankful that she wasn't in any more pain or suffering but I was still gutted. I remember getting home and my neighbour Duane McEwan tried to console me but I broke down in his arms. He's a good mate, a proud Scotsman like my mum was, and they always got on well.

My mum didn't have an easy life, she worked in a lot of low paid jobs like cleaning but she loved it and did it well. She had some good mates and was happy in her own little bubble. Her friend Rose, who'd been like a second mum to me growing up, was another big help and support in those final weeks before she passed away.

She loved her TV and was always happy as long as she had one. In later years we used to see her two or three times a week and she was a brilliant nana to the kids. My youngest Vinny always talks about her, he's got a really good memory for specific things and can remember places he went with her which is nice.

She was always there in the background, most grandparents don't have their grandkids for four or five days at a time but she'd have them all. She'd take them to work and all over the place on her own. She was so invested and doted on them. They all used to stay over a lot which was nice because it gave Simone and I a break and they all have good memories with her.

I remember being stood with her watching one of Taelor's football games not long before she died. I've always thought he's better technically than I was and he works harder too. I mentioned that to her and she just looked at me and said, "John you don't realise how good you were." She was a character and left her mark on the world. I inherited her personality and I'm proud of it.

I suffered my own health scare in early 2019. I kept getting headaches and Simone kept telling me to go to the doctors. I went in the end and they told me my blood pressure was sky high and that I needed to go to hospital straight away. I got the shock of my life when the doctor came out with all the results after they'd done some tests. He knelt down in front of me and said: "Right young man, I've got some news to tell you."

I'm sat there thinking "This is it, I'm dying!"

It wasn't as bad as I'd feared but he told me that if I hadn't come in I would probably have had a heart attack or stroke within a week. My blood pressure was way too high and it had damaged my kidneys. They told me I had hypertension and borderline stage three or four kidney disease. I had too much potassium in my urine which can cause all kinds of problems apparently.

Apparently you have veins in your kidneys and instead of being full mine have gaps in them and need filling up.

I've since been confirmed as stage four so ever since I've been on a course of tablets to control it and will be for the rest of my life. If it gets worse I might need a transplant but so far everything is under control. I think Andy Cole went through something similar a few years ago and apparently it's something that black or mixed-race people are at higher risk of. It can be a Jamaican thing apparently so could be hereditary from my dad's side of the family.

It may have been caused by a build-up of pressure in my head from what I had to deal with over the years with my tics and twitching alongside all the pressure from my football career. I suppressed a lot and it's damaged me in the long run. It may have just come to a head and thankfully I went and got checked out before it got even more serious.

They say stress is a silent killer. I have a pump to check my blood pressure every other day and it's perfect at the moment so as long as things continue as they are I should be alright. I'm more settled in my life now too, there's not really any pressure to deal with other than feeding and clothing my kids.

You can't take life for granted and you just don't realise how fragile your health can be. If I'd have been one of those old school blokes I wouldn't have gone to the doctors, kept going and probably died. Fortunately I re-evaluated my life and looked at what was important and woke up. It was scary at the time and touch wood everything stays as it is going forward.

At the beginning of 2020 me and Simone decided to call it a day and part ways. There was no bad feeling, we were just different people at different stages of our lives. We still get on and she's a great mum to the kids, not many people would have been able to cope with having a baby at 19 whilst trying to progress a career as well as she did.

We don't hate each other and it's just about making sure the kids are happy really.

# TWO JOHN O'KANES

I'M A MANCHESTER UNITED FAN. I SPENT nearly ten years at the club playing hundreds of games for them at all levels and was lucky enough to play for the first team, it's in me. I love the club and I love what it stands for. I've supported them since the day I signed in 1989 and it's in my blood now. There's nothing I can do about that and I have a passion for it that maybe I didn't always have when I was there as a player. Which is weird in a way.

It's been a big part of my life and still is. I watch every game and try to get to as many as I can but I don't have a direct relationship with the club. I usually take my lad Taelor but Ruby has been too and I'm due to take Vinny at some point.

As fans we were spoilt for 20 years but the last few years have been more difficult since the gaffer retired with problems on the pitch and behind the scenes. The likes of Ed Woodward are very unpopular with the majority of the fans but in the eyes of the owners he's making them money so holds a lot of power.

I've been very outspoken against the Glazer family because I don't agree with their running of the club. They put the club in a lot of debt when they bought it like it was a self-certified mortgage - only the club is paying back the mortgage! You've got to hand it to them, business-wise what they've done is amazing. They've used the club to do countless commercial deals whilst taking their dividend every year and not investing any of their own money into it, like the owners at Chelsea and City have. It's not run like a football club, it's a business to them and all they care about is the bottom line.

The fact we turnover hundreds of millions of pounds but are reluctant to spend money shows something isn't right. Transfers are a big issue, we seem to have trouble attracting players and getting deals over the line with a lot of speculation being thrown about which doesn't actually materialise into anything apart from clicks on social media.

It's the injustice that's riled me, it's always taken something like that to ignite my passion like it sometimes did when I was playing. I know the club have spent hundreds of millions on transfers but the Glazers have taken a huge amount of cash out of it and if we were allowed to spend our own money there's no reason why United wouldn't be competing with the best in Europe.

There has been a massive 'Green and Gold' campaign against them that has been going since 2005 when they took over. The club was successful in the next few years afterwards but I think the gaffer knew he wouldn't be able to rebuild his team that won the league in 2013 because they weren't prepared to spend the money to do it. It looks like they don't want to put any money into the club but they're more than happy to take it out. It's scandalous.

The campaign has really come back to the fore in the last few years but I don't think they're going anywhere any time soon. We're always going to be in debt until someone buys us for billions and there aren't many people in the world who can afford that.

I'm just a fan at the end of the day and I support Manchester United and not the name above the door. Some people on Twitter accuse me of being too negative but I'm just being honest which is something a lot of former players can't be, for whatever reason. I get a lot of stick for it on social media but I don't care.

I just want the best for the club. The same goes with the manager, I played a few reserve games with Ole Gunnar Solskjaer. He was a nice lad but we didn't mix too much because we were in separate dressing rooms at the Cliff. I've no affiliation to him, he's not a mate just another former colleague which allows me to judge him on what he is as a manager.

He's a legend because of the goal he scored in the 1999 Champions League final but he was probably lucky to get the job in the first place and wouldn't have been my first choice because there were more qualified coaches out there. I think the hierarchy at Old Trafford knew that when they made the appointment they could hide behind him and the fans wouldn't turn on him because of the memories he gave them as a player. He's a safer option for them and the opposite of Jose Mourinho who was very outspoken, Ole never really gets riled by anything and doesn't bite in press conferences or criticise them. It's divided the fans with some refusing to go against him because he's a nice bloke and was a good player for the club but then there's the others who want better for the club regardless.

I'm not really in the 'In' or 'Out' camp as such, he needs backing financially with the right players brought in but I do wonder if he's been given a project by the owners to trim the wage bill and invest in youth to help save money instead of the club going out and purchasing elite players in their prime. That's what's needed for us to challenge but the ambition just seems to be to get in the top four whilst spending as little as possible.

He's learning on the job so needs a higher level of

experience in his back-room staff, Mike Phelan is a good start but I think he needs someone like Rene Meulensteen in there and a good defensive coach. It shows in the way we play because tactically he has been found wanting at times and we've struggled to establish any sort of pattern of play or style, mostly relying on counter attacking or moments to win games. The Bruno Fernandes signing could save him but I think we're too dependent on him or a flash of brilliance from the forwards.

With team selections he has his blind spots like all managers do and you can see the self-preservation there when things aren't going well or in big games with two holding midfielders. He's won a few big games, got to semi-finals and in the top four but the next step is for the club to win a trophy with him having been in the job for nearly three years. We seem to come up short when it really matters, so there's a bit of a mental block there which is a worrying pattern and needs to improve going forward if we're going to compete with City who seem to have a better standard of coaching and recruitment.

It's going to take time for it to reset which is what's been needed and apparently behind the scenes that's what's happening. You can see what he's trying to do by getting the attitude at the club right and back to the way it used to be. I've heard he's ruthless and has a nasty side to him. I got told a story about him being stood watching a youth team game and one of the United players didn't celebrate when they scored a goal and Solskjaer went ballistic and ordered that he was brought off immediately. He's weeded out a lot of players, there's still a few that need to go and more technical players who can handle the ball need to be brought in and ultimately time will tell.

My views on the way the club is run got me into a spat on Twitter with my old mate Gary Neville when he made out there was no point in fans protesting against the owners and it got personal.

"Are there 2 John O'Kanes? The one I knew that cowered at the thought of giving his all for the club and was unprofessional whilst wearing the shirt and this one who is a Twitter warrior and represents the fans with all his heart. Can't be the same bloke surely!"

It's a couple of years ago now but it still riles me because he doesn't know anything of what I had to go through. He doesn't know the facts about my life, he just made a snap judgement. It's as if he judged me as a person on not making it at Manchester United, something which isn't unusual, and just because he played hundreds of games in my position it doesn't make him a better person than me. You need to be a good player to even get in the door at United and I was there for nine years so must have done something right.

I played in the first team and in my eyes even if it was just for one minute I made it but there's this mentality in football that if you've not played hundreds of games at the highest level and got loads of medals then you're a failure. You see players being held in such high regard for what they did in the game but at the end of the day it's just kicking a ball around. They've not cured cancer or ended world famine and they've made a hell of a lot of money from it. Fair play to them but it doesn't make them a better person than the average bloke on the street because at the end of the day football is a form of entertainment, it's not real life.

From Gary's point of view he probably knows I had the ability and thinks I should have gone on to play hundreds of games for United and won England caps. I didn't because sometimes life doesn't work like that and all I know is I've worked in a profession where I've helped people's lives who are vulnerable be that little bit better. Meanwhile he's been successful in football and outside of it, it depends what you want from life and I'd rather spend time with my kids than be on TV every night. He has done plenty of good things like opening his hotels for NHS staff and the homeless but we're completely different people with different paths.

He has his opinions on everything and I enjoy watching him on TV. He's quite black and white and I like the honesty in that but he's just another former colleague and I don't care what he thinks of me. He went personal and there are things I could have come back at him with but I didn't. I also thought it was funny how it took the Glazers trying to launch the European Super League a couple of years later for him to publicly speak out against them, maybe because it would have impacted his own club. The owners showed their true colours in trying to do that and if more former players with his influence spoke out against them it could speed up their exit from the club.

At the end of the day the work I did in care and my three kids are my medals. They're my legacy and Manchester United will probably be around forever and my name will always be associated with them.

I returned to Old Trafford in 2017 when United played Crystal Palace on the last day of the season with some of the other lads from our youth team to honour Eric Harrison and Nobby Stiles. It was mostly the fringe players who turned up and we went on the pitch, sat in the director's box then went back to Fergie's office for a drink afterwards.

Simone was a bit tipsy when she met us there after the game and starting laying into Fergie about me. She was chatting to him in the players' lounge and I could hear her having a right go at him and Jim Ryan about the mental health stuff I had going on: "Why was he never given any help? None of you ever helped him." It was funny in a way and I had to laugh because she was sticking up for me. When she'd finished I had a chat with the gaffer and found myself apologising.

"Boss, I'm sorry I didn't give everything for you. I should have done more than I did. I knew I was good enough but my head wasn't right when I was here."

"John, don't worry about it. You were good enough, it just wasn't for you. It just doesn't work out for everybody and it's one of those things. You don't need to apologise."

I'd been waiting for 20 years to say that to him and it felt like closure. We had a good chat and I remember talking to him about who United should sign that summer. I asked him about Harry Kane but he was set on Dele Alli. They were both on fire at the time, "Who would you buy right now if you were still manager?"

"I'd have Alli all day, John."

I've been retired from football for about 15 years now. It gave me some good memories, particularly at the start when I was growing up, of having a good laugh and enjoying myself. I met some great people and it gave me so many good experiences in life that so many people don't get to live for a second. I definitely took it for granted but while you're in there you don't think of anything else outside that bubble. I wish I understood what I do now but when you're going through it you're just a kid and you think you know it all.

Do I have any regrets? Yeah I could have probably handled a few situations differently and bitten my tongue a bit more but in a way I'm proud that I spoke up and stayed true to myself. I've always taken people how they treated me no matter what their standing within the game. I never took life too seriously, that's what probably came across in people's perceptions of me that I was lazy and didn't really care but it's just in my DNA.

I had the ability to make it at the top level, few of my team-mates would argue with that, but it was the mental side of the game where I fell down. Dealing with things like pressure, my background and the stuff going on in my head meant I was lacking in that area. It's like any time I went for a trial, my ability would kick in and people could see it but once you're through the door it's the mental strength to deal with what you're going to come up against that keeps you there.

I always had one foot out of the door in football because deep down I knew something wasn't right, I didn't feel totally comfortable there and that's why I quit early. I stayed in as long as I could but by the end I'd just burnt out and knew that there was something else I had to do.

Having said that, I battled a lot to have the career I did have and you have to be mentally tough to do that. I said to Robbo a while ago that if I'd have had his head and the stability he had with his family I'd have been a different player but we're all made up differently and have our own paths. I had a mental disability which used up a lot of resource to the extent that there wasn't much left and I was relying on my skill to blag it. I could have been released by United at 18 or even younger but I managed to battle and suppress my demons to have a career in the game.

I guess I'm an example that anyone who's on the spectrum or has any other form of disability can still achieve in sport and life because I managed to play football at a high standard for a sustained period and if the awareness around it had been there at the time I could have gone even further. I've only been diagnosed as being on the spectrum in the last few years but I wasn't surprised, it just confirmed what I'd always known. There'll be millions of people out there who struggle with something and I can relate to it because I am one of them.

It's a tough world and despite some people's perceptions you have to be mentally strong to cope with something like that. Even now, it's a daily routine for me of not putting myself in certain situations that cause me too much stress or anxiety but you have to keep going and get help if you need it. Small goals can be huge ones but if you believe in yourself you can achieve anything and never be afraid of who you are.

I was from a council estate in Bilborough and I played for Manchester United, the biggest club in the world. I played in the Premier League, at Wembley and I've met Nelson Mandela. I suppose I didn't take it that seriously. It's some achievement really and nobody can take it away from me. I had a good run and I can't lie; I'd have been overjoyed to have been in that 1999 treble team but it's not the be-all and end-all. I was a professional footballer and not many people can say that but it's just a game at the end of the day – a small part of my life.

If one of my kids ever went into professional sport I'm definitely a good soundboard for it because I know exactly what's needed. I've lived every different part of football. They know what their dad did but my house isn't some sort of shrine to my career. They've seen videos or me on TV when old games are replayed and a few pictures here and there. I've got a few bits but they're tucked away or in the loft.

I'm probably the happiest I've ever been and there's not much I really need in life. I enjoy watching United which has turned into a hobby itself; I enjoy my golf and try to get out for a round as much as I can which also helps me keep in touch with a few ex-team-mates.

I've got a nice little circle of mates and I still see Goughy, Robbo and Andy Bower fairly regularly. We go back a long way and they're probably the three people who know me best. I'm also in a fantasy football league and WhatsApp group with a group of lads I've met through all walks of life. I've mentioned some of them already but in no particular order there's Dave Meikle, Mark Hacker, Sean Watts, Joe McMillan, Ashley Burd, Andy Morris, my son Taelor, Haris Latif, Iain Reedy, Luke Alemanno, Declan Ferry, Gianpaolo Vignali, Daniel Waterhouse, Haroon Latif, Tom McDermott, Jamie Farrell and Owen Dawson.

I get ridiculous banter in there, it's brutal but all good fun and another way for the lads to share the latest videos that are doing the rounds on the internet. Being a former player doesn't tend to help me with fantasy football though and I get hammered every week for my selections. I usually start off well and end up near the bottom, I'm known as the 'grim reaper' because most players I pick tend to get injured.

I'm an ordinary guy with an ordinary house on an ordinary street. I enjoy the simple things like gardening and tending to my plants or playing with my kids. I like watching them play football or do gymnastics, it's just about taking those little moments and enjoying them as much as I can. I just want a simple life, always have.

I had my lightbulb moment when I was about 30, a lot of people get stuck in that routine of going to work and chasing money. I get it because people have bills to pay and families to feed. It's not always possible but if you can somehow get away from that and realise there's more to life. People always couple success with being happy but it's not always true, you could be gone tomorrow and all that striving or worrying about meeting deadlines is for nothing. People might grieve for a while but the world moves on and you're quickly forgotten about.

I've found peace with myself mentally, something I never had whilst I was playing and I'm more comfortable in my own skin than I've ever been. I was always battling something or someone but now I'm older I just feel like I can breathe and a big weight's been lifted.

I wouldn't rule out going back into football in some capacity, I was lined up to do some scouting for Swindon Town when Richie Wellens was manager there, when you've played the game it's easy to read players and know their strengths and weaknesses so I was looking forward to it. With my luck though the Covid-19 pandemic meant that I was unable to start and then of course Wellens got the job at Salford City of all clubs so that was the end of that. At the moment I'm busy enough being a taxi for my kids and taking them all to play football on a Saturday which is a job in itself, I enjoy doing it though. After 15 years in care and a similar amount of time in football before that I've decided to take some time out, although I feel like I still have something to give or that there's something I'm destined to do in life.

As for the future, I've no solid plans and don't know what I'm going to be doing next week. I'm like a paper bag blowing in the wind just willing to go wherever it may take me. Look at the jobs I've had since I finished playing, we all have our own paths to follow and the fact I used to play football for a living will never define me as a person. Life is about experiences and I've made mistakes but I've lived.

In a way, Gary Neville was right. There are two John O'Kane's; the first spent about 15 years living in a superficial bubble where he didn't really belong and ended a long time ago. The second worked in one of the toughest industries in society to help make people's lives a bit better and is a dad to three great kids. I know which one I'm most proud of…

*I'll keep on moving*
*Things are bound to be improving these days*
*These days-*
*These days I sit on corner stones*
*And count the time in quarter tones to ten, my friend*
*Don't confront me with my failures*
*I had not forgotten them*

Lyrics from 'These Days' by Jackson Browne

## Paul Gough

*I've known John since we signed for Manchester United as schoolboys and lived in digs on Bury New Road. We stayed mates after I left and I followed his career right the way through.*

*He had an amazing career at face value, but I think it's fair to say he didn't reach his potential, not because of his technical ability and certainly not because of his commitment, it's just his personality didn't suit the game of that era and certain managers were too quick to make their minds up about him.*

*It wasn't that John wasn't bothered or he sacked it off, he definitely gave 100%, it's just he wasn't motivated to respond to that competitive environment where everything is a race, super competitive and coaches getting into you all the time. That gave rise to people saying he didn't care and it followed him around a bit.*

*He definitely played 20 years too early and I think with the way attitudes have changed if he had been playing in this generation he would have had a better career. Nowadays most clubs employ a sports psychologist who'd probably just do a little bit of work with him and they'd get an understanding of what made him tick. Once they did that and unlocked his motivation then he's a Premier League player from start to finish.*

*Most people always give excuses as to why they didn't make it in the game. They blame injury, the coach or whatever else and I've never heard any of that from John about the way his career turned out. There doesn't seem to be any bitterness or regret there whatsoever in all of the years I've known him. I think it's just part of his personality, he always seems content and whatever comes his way, he just seems to crack on with it.*

*I think that's one of his great qualities and he's one of my favourite people. Today I still count him as one of my best mates.*

## Andy Bower

*Me and John have had some good times together and still have some great banter but I don't see as much of him as I'd like. He's made a lot of friends through football but I think his strongest friendships are with myself, Goughy and Robbo.*

*I think he's happier now than he has been for a long time so fair play to him.*

## Steve Robinson

*I think John knows if he needs somebody I'd be there for him. We see each other every couple of months, we've both got families and kids so it's not as much as it used to be. We played golf together a few weeks ago and he walked off the course after nine holes because it wasn't going his way – typical John.*

*He's a good lad and a nice guy. He had a lot going for him but ultimately I think he's happier now when he gets a pair of trousers for £11 from Primark than the £300 ones he used to wear playing for Manchester United. I think he's in a happier place now.*

*There's thousands of players out there who would give their right arm to have John O'Kane's career. He was ten times more talented than me and ten times better looking too…*

# CAREER STATS

<u>Manchester United 1989 – 1998</u>

'B' team – 23 appearances
'A' team – 70 appearances
Reserves – 96 appearances, 7 goals.
First team – 7 appearances, 0 goals.

<u>HONOURS:</u>

1992 FA Youth Cup Winner
Pontins Reserve League winner – 1993/94, 1995/96, 1996/97

<u>Loan spells:</u>

Wimbledon 1995 – 3 appearances, 0 goals.
Bury 1996/97 – 13 appearances, 3 goals. Division 2 winner.
Bradford City – 1997 – 6 appearances, 0 goals.

<u>Everton 1998-1999</u>
17 appearances, 0 goals.

<u>Loan spell</u>

Burnley 1998 – 8 appearances, 0 goals.

<u>Bolton Wanderers 1999-2001</u>
46 appearances, 3 goals.

Blackpool 2001 – 2003

67 appearances, 4 goals.

HONOURS: 2002 LDV Vans Trophy winner

Hyde United 2003 – 2006
116 appearances, 9 goals.

HONOURS:

Northern Premier League Division One winner – 2003/04
Northern Premier League Chairman's Cup – 2003/04
Northern Premier League – 2004/05
Manchester Premier Cup – 2004/05